D0626751

A
Couple's
Journey
with
God

Bill & Pam Farrel

HARVEST HOUSE PUBLISHERS
EUGENE, OREGON

Cover by Left Coast Design, Portland, Oregon
Cover photo © Petr Malyshev / Shutterstock

Bill and Pam Farrel are represented by the literary agency of Alive Communications, Inc., 7680 Goddard Street, Ste #200, Colorado Springs, CO 80920.

A COUPLE'S JOURNEY WITH GOD

Published by Harvest House Publishers
Eugene, Oregon 97402
www.harvesthousepublishers.com

ISBN 978-0-7369-4542-4 (pbk.)
ISBN 978-0-7369-4543-1 (eBook)

Printed in China

12 13 14 15 16 17 18 19 20 / FC-GLD / 10 9 8 7 6 5 4 3 2 1

To
Brock & Hannah
and
Zach & Caleigh,

Your love stories have already inspired
others to love more like God.
We trust you will continue to add to the
legacy of love we have layered into your lives,
and we are grateful to God for bringing such
amazing daughters-in-law into our family.
As couples, keep loving each other with God's
power and God will give you an epic love story.
Enjoy your journey of love!

For the LORD is good and his love endures forever;
his faithfulness continues through all generations
(Psalm 100:5).

We will not hide them from their descendants;
we will tell the next generation
the praiseworthy deeds of the LORD,
his power, and the wonders he has done
(Psalm 78:4).

And to our Harvest House publishing family,
and our editor, Kathleen Kerr.

Bless you for building love into couples on their journeys.
May God bless each of you on your journey of love.

Day 1

Sentimental Journey

*Please grant success to the journey on
which I have come.*
GENESIS 24:42

We know something about the journeys couples take together. We have been happily married
for over 32 years, and we both have over a million
frequent flyer miles on our favorite airline. We have
crisscrossed the globe speaking and teaching on
marriage for over 20 of those years.

Travel is an excellent tutor to help you hone
your marriage skills. The irritations commonplace
to travel—the jet lag, the unpredictability of your
next meal, the delays and cancellations, the constant

transitions while carrying loads of baggage—are a good reflection of the average couple's marriage but compressed and accelerated to jet speed.

Just like you might need help from a seasoned flight attendant to get that overstuffed bag into an overhead luggage compartment, we're here to lend you some of the wisdom we've gathered over the miles:

A great marriage is like a bullet train. The speed rail options between large metro cities like New York and Boston offer nonstop service, letting you get on and go straight through to your destination. When you said, "Till death do us part," you were committing to a traveling companion for the duration. The person you start marriage with is supposed to be the same person you usher into heaven. That is God's ideal. The journey of love is easier and richer if you make it all the way together.

A great marriage is like a cruise. We have been guest speakers on a few cruises, and we love the opportunity to stop at every port to go sightseeing. No one is in a hurry—a cruise ship is not a jet ski! A great marriage builds in time for romance, time to slow down, and time to enjoy the company of your mate. If you and your spouse factor in time to "cruise" together, love will remain strong because you will have time to remember why you first fell in love!

A great marriage is like an overseas flight. When traveling great distances it's likely that you will have to make several connections, transferring planes or airlines. Many times the unexpected happens—canceled flights, rerouting, and lost luggage are commonplace hassles. To be a successful traveler you have to be flexible and adaptable. You have to have the ability to keep a positive attitude when you are tired, starving, and displaced. Marriage is like that. There are so many unknowns on life's route. Every couple deals with typical transitions like becoming parents or midlife aging, but there may be surprises along the way like illness, financial worry, or prodigal kids. These surprises might make you feel like you're stranded in unknown territory. But if you're able to adapt on the go, you'll get to travel to exciting places and make great marriage memories!

A great marriage is like a backpacking hike. Sometimes marriage feels like it's all an uphill climb—

Day 2

A Life Well Lived

*This is to my Father's glory, that you
bear much fruit, showing yourselves
to be my disciples.*
JOHN 15:8

We live near the mountain town of Julian, California, which is known for its apple farms, apple festivals, and apple pies! A whole economy is built from good fruit. Have you ever picked fruit? I (Pam) grew up on a farm and we had some apple trees on that property. Each fall it was the job of the children to harvest those apples, so I was an apple picker and inspector. Some of the trees produced fruit that was luscious, sweet, and bountiful, filling our bushel baskets up to the brim with tasty treats. Some of the other trees, however, gave a smaller harvest, or fruit that was malformed and misshapen. Some trees didn't bear any apples at all!

A ministry colleague said to us recently, "When I look at your lives, all the wise decisions and the fruit they bore in your marriage, family, and community, I think, 'That is a life well lived.'" Wow! That is one of the nicest compliments we could ever receive. It was especially encouraging because one of our daily prayers as a couple is, "Help us be so tied into You, Jesus, that we bear lasting fruit." When we look at our children and our ministry, we can tell that our prayer is being answered!

Jesus talks about the kinds of fruit one can elect to produce:

> No good tree bears bad fruit, nor does a bad tree bear good fruit. Each tree is recognized by its own fruit. People do not pick figs from thornbushes, or grapes from briers. A good man brings good things out of the good stored up in his heart, and an evil man brings evil things out of the evil stored up in his heart. For the mouth speaks what the heart is full of (Luke 6:43-45).

So what is the difference between a tree that produces good fruit and one that produces bad? And how can you develop a relationship that produces good fruit?

The roots: A tree that produces good fruit is rooted in the person of God. God created the two of you, so He knows how to make your relationship work best. Begin by giving control over to Jesus. Let Christ sit in the driver's seat of your life and love.

The trunk: A fruit-producing tree has a wide, strong base developed by long years of growing next to the streams of living water referred to in Psalm 1:3: "That person is like a tree planted by streams of water, which yields its fruit in season and whose leaf does not wither—whatever they do prospers." All the work you do as a couple rests on and stems from this solid base.

The branches: A fruit-bearing love will also have the goal of pleasing the other over yourself. The best marriages have a "Let's do what is best for you" attitude. As you both seek what is best for the other, the branches of love will grow plentifully and strong.

The leaves: Like the foliage of a fruit-bearing tree, love will shelter you both from the harshness of the world. Just as vegetation is a sanctuary to the fruit from the scorching sun and the freezing storms, so kindness is a shelter that will protect your love from the cruel realities of life. We suggest you try to do something kind, thoughtful, or romantic each day, and together you will produce a love that flourishes and produces the fruit of community, respect, success at work, children who grow to be leaders, financial security, and other more intangible blessings like hope, joy, and cherished memories.

Conversely, as you might guess, the tree with little or no fruit (or "evil fruit," as the passage suggests) is one based on narcissism, selfishness, and self-absorption. As a couple, it is easy to say, "Bless us two and to heck with you." Couples can live in selfish isolation. Worse still, we have seen couples so caught up with attaining the trappings of wealth, power, and worldly success that when one of them had a crisis in their health or an emotional trauma, the other simply cast off the spouse who was a shackle to his or her dreams. They left their mate sitting wounded, bruised, and battered by the roadside. Self-absorbed couples also produce self-centered children who have little or no time for their parents. Be prepared to handle old age on your own if you spent your family-raising years chasing the almighty dollar! Now, money itself isn't the problem—money's just a tool. However, our attitude toward money and the accumulation of worldly goods can become a consuming pursuit, and Jesus wants that place of priority in your heart.

So what kind of fruit do you want your love to produce? Each day we walk with Jesus we increase the possibilities of gaining the fruit-filled life we long for. God has bushel baskets full of blessings He longs to give to the two of you. Are there any changes or course corrections you want to make in your life to gain them?

Lord, make our relationship one that reflects Your heart and Your values. Help us produce ample good fruit in the lives of those around us. Amen.

Baby, I Want You!

*Awake, O north wind, and come, wind of the
south; make my garden breathe out fragrance,
let its spices be wafted abroad.
May my beloved come into his garden and
eat its choice fruits!*

SONG OF SONGS 4:16 NASB

Every couple needs a code word! This is a word
or phrase that lets your mate know you are interested in intimacy with him or her. Hey, this isn't our
idea, it's God's! In Song of Solomon we see the bride
flirting to her groom with metaphors:

My beloved has gone down to his garden, to the
beds of balsam, to pasture his flock in the gardens

and gather lilies. I am my beloved's and my beloved is mine, he who pastures his flock among the lilies (Song of Songs 6:2-3 NASB).

Song of Songs is written metaphorically to shelter it from young eyes. To protect the innocence of the next generation, only adults understood the double meaning of the text. For example, anytime the word *garden* or *flowers* (like the lilies in the verses above) are mentioned, it is a word picture for female sex organs. Here the bride is inviting her husband to have "red-hot monogamy" with her.

Here are a few of our favorite code word stories:

One clergy couple shared with us how their code word evolved. They were the parents of toddlers and life was more than a little bit stressful! The husband's sister, who was single, volunteered to watch the kids for an evening so her brother and sister-in-law could go on a date. Most of the date was spent talking through life issues as the couple sat on a riverbank and fed the ducks.

When they returned to the sister-in-law's to retrieve the children, she asked, "So how'd it go?"

Her brother said, "We just talked and fed the ducks."

"Fed the ducks, huh?" She smiled, thinking it was his code word for enjoying intimacy with his wife.

The dad gathered the children and headed out to the car to meet his wife. After the kids were tucked into bed, he explained how his sister thought *feeding the ducks* was a code for sex. His wife grinned and replied, "So, want to go feed the ducks?" For years now, this couple has been happily "feeding the ducks."

While speaking in the Bible Belt of the USA, one meeting planner emceed a kind of dating game. One question was, "What would be your husband's favorite date?" The first woman answered, "We might go out to dinner, but we would 'come home early!'" The second woman said, "We might go to a movie, but I'm pretty sure we would 'come home early!'" The emcee brought the husbands back in to answer the same question. The last of the husbands answered, "We might catch a movie and dinner, but I am pretty sure we would come home early, light a fire in the fireplace, and light a fire on the couch!" I learned that day that if I heard a Southern Belle say, "We need to come home early," somewhere there would be a Southern gentleman with a smile on his face!

One couple decided that every time they made love, they would put a dollar in a bank to save toward their second honeymoon. Often he'd walk in from work and say, "I've got a dollar!" She would respond, "I know how to spend it!" Then off they'd go to the bedroom. This ritual happened week after week for years. If a business meeting would turn boring, all she had to do to end the meeting was to slide a dollar bill across the table—business meeting *over!* Year after year they traded dollar bills back and forth, enjoyed satisfying sexual intimacy, and watched the money added up in the bank. When their fiftieth wedding anniversary came around they went to Hawaii for several weeks. They stayed in all the best places, ate at the nicest restaurants, and enjoyed the most exciting activities. At the end of the trip their daughter picked them up at the airport. As she tells the story, "At baggage claim Daddy pulled out his wallet, took out a dollar, and said to Mama, 'Want to start saving for Cancun?'"

Got a dollar?

Better Than Vitamins

Will you not revive us again, that your people
may rejoice in you? Show us your unfailing
love, Lord, and grant us your salvation.
PSALM 85:6-7

Revived! Just the word conjures up images of spas, a massage, healthy food, and a long Sunday afternoon nap in the sun. The wellness industry is mammoth. If you go to a newsstand, you will see numerous magazines promoting good health. If you head to the health food store you will find shelves upon shelves of health supplements and vitamins. But God has gone one step better and built in a wellness booster for married couples: *sex.* In our book *Red-Hot Monogamy*, we give some scientific stats that back up God's great plan for rejuvenation within marriage:

Sex within the context of marriage is good for your emotional and physical wellbeing. Sex raises the endorphin level so it makes you happier. Sex burns calories! "According to the calorie counter on the Health Status website, an hour of sex burns 250 calories, the same amount as an hour of walking. To better put this number in perspective, sixty minutes of sleeping burns 55 calories, and an hour of running burns 800. Assuming that one did not make any alterations in his or her diet, by engaging in an hour of sex every day, one would lose a pound every two weeks."[1] (Finally, a diet plan we can succeed at!)

"Kissing burns calories, too. Professor Bryant Stamford, PhD of the University of Louisville, postulates that a deep, passionate kiss may double your basic metabolic rate and burn as many as two calories a minute. Do the math. Kissing for 15 minutes burns approximately 30 calories. If one were to kiss passionately for 15 minutes that might lead to other calorie burning activities!"[2]

Of course, sex does not qualify as the cornerstone of your aerobic workout program, but it is a great addition. We like what Janet Lee of GymAmerica .com has to say about how many calories are burned during sex:

"Let's put it this way: If you're planning to make sex a part of an already active lifestyle, great. But if you're relying on it to lose weight or tone up, you'd need to spend hours a day in the sack. According to the energy expenditure tables compiled by exercise physiologists and found in the *Health and Fitness Instructors Handbook* (Human Kinetics, 1997), sex burns anywhere from 60 to 120 (the lower range for foreplay and the upper range for particularly vigorous sex) calories an hour for a 130-lb. woman and 77 to 155 calories an hour for a 170-lb. man. Considering that running burns around 600 calories an hour, you can see that sex is not the most efficient mode of weight loss. In fact, foreplay takes about the same amount of energy as sitting around on the couch, and a more rousing session that might wake up the neighbors is still only the equivalent of a slow walk. But really, who's counting?"[3]

Solomon and his wife understood this principle: Sex is the secret to revival in marriage. Even without all the scientific studies, they, like untold numbers of married couples over the ages, grasped the simple fact that they felt better after intimacy. Solomon's wife compared sex with her husband to her need for food: "Strengthen me with raisins," she said, and "refresh me with apples, for I am faint with love" (Song of Songs 2:5).

If you are married, talk through your schedule with your spouse. Are you living in a rhythm that gives you plenty of opportunity for feeling revived by love? Do you need to slow your pace, set up a rendezvous, or cultivate a romantic atmosphere? If you are looking forward to marriage, cultivate your friendship with romantic dates (without sex until marriage) so you lay a stable, loving environment for your future marriage.

Song of Songs has often been interpreted on two levels. The first is as the love story of a husband and a wife, and the second is as a metaphor or picture of God's love for His people. On either level, it becomes apparent that relationship is revival.

Lord, help us to love in a way that revives our love and marriage. Amen.

Day 5

Bicycle Built for Two

For we walk by faith, not by sight.
2 Corinthians 5:7 nasb

When we were still newlyweds, I (Pam) worked as a special education aide. Bill and I helped Anton, a blind student, experience as many physical activities as possible. He dreamed of things like baseball, bike riding, and even going on a swing or slide. One day, we rented a bicycle built for two. I got on the front while Bill helped Anton climb on. Bill steadied the bike, then I pedaled away to the sound of Anton's giggles and happy squeals. He was pedaling in complete darkness. Anton was showing great faith—exactly the kind of faith that we wives are sometimes called by God to live out.

When God called Bill to attend Talbot Seminary to become a pastor, it meant moving this farm girl to the heart of Los Angeles. I wasn't even sure God existed in LA! But just as Anton trusted me as I pedaled and steered into one of the best adventures of his young life, I was being called to climb on back of the bicycle built for two as Bill wheeled us to California's urban jungle to prepare for a lifetime of service to God.

I'll admit that I felt a little like Sarai, Abram's wife. God had called out to Abram and said, "Go from your country, your people and your father's household to the land I will show you" (Genesis 12:1).

Can you imagine the conversation that must have followed?

"Sarai, God told me we are moving."

"Moving! Where?"

"Don't know. He will tell us."

"Well, when do we leave?"

"Now."

To Sarai's credit, she went! How many of us would have shown that kind of trust and obedience? How many of us squelch the hopes and dreams of our mate? When your man shares his clear call from God, how do you react? With skepticism? Anger? Naysaying? And when your wife is offered an opportunity to spread her wings and soar, do you clip them? Trust God to take you *both* on an adventure as you each succeed in whatever calling He has for you. He knows you are a team, and if you walk together through the doors God is opening for you, you can trust that you'll find blessings there!

Sarai knew that her husband desired to walk with God and obey Him. She trusted God and followed her man, and in the new land she was blessed with her long-awaited miracle son, Isaac. When you trust God, pedaling by faith into what might seem to be the dark unknown, you might just have the ride of your life!

Hop on!

Lord, let us not be fearful of the adventure. Father, You are in the driver's seat and we trust You even when we can't see the path ahead. Amen.

Can You Hear Me Now?

My dear brothers and sisters, take note of this:
Everyone should be quick to listen, slow to
speak and slow to become angry.
JAMES 1:19

The key principle in promoting intimacy is giving your spouse permission to share at a vulnerable level. If your spouse senses the go-ahead to share, new information will emerge. This new information will lead you to a better understanding of your spouse and the emotions that motivate his or her actions and decisions. The listening skills that grant permission to your spouse are:

- *Repeat* back key phrases the other person is saying. Key phrases usually have a feeling word in them ("I am *afraid* we're getting into debt." "She *upset* me." "I am *frustrated* with him."). Look for the word or phrase that denotes a feeling and repeat that part of the sentence.

- *Rephrase* what has been said ("What I'm hearing you saying is…"). Put what your spouse has shared into your own words.

- *Regroup.* Ask for clarification. Is what you heard close to what he or she said? ("So, honey, am I in the ballpark?" or "Is this what you meant?")

- *Reconnect.* Try to relate his or her feelings to your own experience. ("Could the way you are feeling be a little like the way I felt when…?") Try to compare something you have been through to the situation they are trying to communicate to you. The circumstances might be very different but your feelings and emotions about the situation might be very similar. What you are trying to establish is a connection that reaches from heart to heart.

Jesus thought listening was a priority too. He started many sentences with, "Whoever has ears, let them hear," "Listen!" or "Listen carefully to what I am about to tell you."

And God commanded that we listen up too! During the Transfiguration, Jesus was joined by Moses and Elijah. All of a sudden "a bright cloud covered them, and a voice from the cloud said, 'This is my Son, whom I love; with him I am well pleased. Listen to him!'" (Matthew 17:5).

Jesus also flatly stated listening was vital: "My sheep listen to my voice; I know them, and they follow me" (John 10:27). Are you and your spouse listening so you can hear God's voice?

Check out the Sermon on the Mount in Matthew 5 and read through it together. In it you will hear the rhythm of a leader trying to get the attention of a very needy audience. Jesus continually repeated the phrases *You have heard it said…* and *but I tell you…* There was a twofold reason for this. First, He needed to prove His authority. In those days teachers didn't really teach their own material. They simply quoted other teachers…who were quoting other teachers who came before them. By saying "But I tell you," Jesus was making it clear that He was the primary authority, the head source.

The second reason Jesus often began His sermons this way was that all the teachers sat and gave instruction in the courtyard of the temple. Picture this—many teachers surrounded by small groups of their followers, all packed into the same portico with no microphone. To get the attention of those who were passing by, you needed a great opening line, one that would catch a person's ear! Giving listeners new, fresh, original ways of living and thinking when everyone else was quoting the same old material was just the ticket!

Seems like if Jesus went to all that trouble to make His voice heard, we ought to listen to it! And if Jesus made listening a priority, perhaps we should listen to each other too!

Lord, help us to listen to You and to each other. Help us tune into Your voice so we can hear and follow together. Amen.

Day 7

Coffee?

Above all, love each other deeply, because love covers over a multitude of sins.
1 PETER 4:8

My husband, Bill, loves his coffee. But along with Bill's love of coffee comes a habit that could be very annoying. He can't seem to get the coffee mugs into the dishwasher! I find coffee cups every place imaginable: in the garage, in the car, in the truck, in the closet, on the sidewalk, on the deck and patio, in the shop, in the office, on the stairwell, in the bathroom—you name it, and I have likely found a coffee cup there. It is a good thing that we are authors and speakers because we love collecting the coffee mugs from all the churches we speak at and all the TV and radio shows we appear on—and we need every one of them!

I am not a coffee drinker really. I might drink a nonfat latte now and then, but for the most part coffee makes my heart race, and I prefer that only Bill makes my heart skip a beat! Bill says that I am naturally caffeinated by God, and it takes Bill three cups of coffee just to keep up with my energy. It's a good thing that he has an internal homing device that helps him spot the green awning of a nearby Starbucks!

So how do I handle these differences between us? By learning to appreciate, emancipate, and celebrate them!

Appreciate the difference: Coffee is a part of what makes Bill, well, Bill! One day, as we were preparing to move to a new home, I was doing that last load of dishes and realized it was composed entirely of coffee mugs! Forty-seven of them, to be exact! I was fuming mad and thought, *Dear Jesus, how can such a great, godly, seemingly very capable man not get his coffee mug to the sink?* I knew the dirty mug issue was an underlying negative resentment, and I wanted it out of our relationship. My nagging about the mugs seemed to make little difference in Bill's progress toward getting them to the sink, so I started praying, knowing that the change might have to come from my side of the equation. And God answered by whispering a question to my heart: "Why does Bill like his coffee so much?"

Bill is a hardworking man, Lord. He needs some of that caffeine! I answered in my mind. Then God whispered back, "And isn't it a privilege to be married to a hardworking man?" My answer was a resounding and emphatic, "*Yes!* This world needs more hardworking men!"

Emancipate the difference: I decided to pray for Bill every time I saw one of his empty displaced mugs. Then I extended the blessing prayer and I began to pray anytime I saw a clean mug. And then I extended it still further and began to pray a blessing over Bill when I saw *anyone* with a coffee mug! Do you know how many people carry coffee mugs through airport terminals, as they drive, as they work, on dates, and through their daily lives? A *lot!*

Several websites say that daily coffee drinkers make up nearly 60 percent of our population. That's a lot of blessing to pray over my husband!

I was seeking to apply the principle "love covers over a multitude of sins" (1 Peter 4:8). (No, coffee is not a sin, but Bill's lack of effort to get the mug to the sink could be seen as a character flaw—at least it felt like one to me until I started praying those coffee mug blessing prayers!) I have now embraced the ever-reappearing dirty coffee mug with fond affection. Each one reminds me of my hard-workin' man who requires caffeine to perform all the wonderful acts of service that benefit so many—including me.

Celebrate the difference: We celebrated Bill's fiftieth birthday by having him select and roast his own brand of coffee. It took a whole afternoon to visit a coffee farm, select the beans, roast them to perfection, and then design the label. I knew I had a winning date as he sat, lingered a moment to savor the aroma of his Farrel Family blend of Mountain Thunder Vienna roast, and took a sip. I got to watch a big grin appear on my husband's well-caffeinated soul![4]

God, if my mate does something that drives me crazy, help me look for the upside, the flipside of that thing so I see my spouse the way You see him or her. Help me desire to bless my mate, and give me creative ways to express my love when I am irritated. Amen.

Day 8

Shared Confidence

Never will I leave you; never will I forsake you.
Hebrews 13:5

I (Bill) grew up in a home where many decisions were made out of fear. We limited our contact with others because we were afraid of people. We spent many weekends in the mountains because we were afraid of what might happen in the neighborhood. We avoided opportunities because of the responsibility that came along with leadership. As a result, I struggled with confidence during my adolescent years. I had an internal desire to be a competitive athlete and a successful student. I was afraid, however, of failing. I had a strange sense that I didn't deserve to accomplish what was in my heart.

37

When Pam and I got married, things began to change. It was important that our relationship succeed. It was a mandate to both of us to be good at raising our kids. Together we determined that we would be strong in the face of fear. In this context, Haggai 2 sheds some interesting light on what it takes to be confident when faced with significant challenges. The challenge before the Israelites was the rebuilding of the temple in Jerusalem. Enemies of Israel had torn down the centerpiece of Israel's history and the task of rebuilding would be resisted by intimidating neighbors.

When faced with a daunting challenge, where do you find the confidence to move forward? Here are some tips for gaining strength in the face of fear:

- Remind yourself you are doing the right thing. Honoring God with a temple that was better than the home of any other citizen was vital to the Israelites' attitude. Everyone knew this was the right thing to do. In the same way, cultivating your love is the right thing to do.

- Remind yourself that God is with you. "I am with you...my Spirit remains among you...I will fill the house with glory" (Haggai 2:4-5,7). The greatest source of humble confidence is the presence of God Himself.

- Stay busy with the work. Thinking too much about obstacles is the fastest way to paralysis. Building a family is hard work, and many tasks along the way will appear to be impossible. When you get busy doing what you know is right even when you can't see how it will all work out, things begin to change. Progress raises your confidence and reorients your perspective. Every step forward encourages another step in the same direction. As a result, part of God's encouragement is "Be strong, all you people of the land...and work" (Haggai 2:4).

- Remind yourself of the promises God has already made to you. God is an active partner in life. He consistently adds His strength and influence to the circumstances of our lives. Every challenge we face is easy for Him because all His attributes are limitless. At the right time, He intervenes so that circumstances do not crush us. "But now be strong...for I am with you...In a little while I will once more shake the heavens and the earth, the sea and the dry land...And in this place I will grant peace" (Haggai 2:4,6,9).

By focusing on God—not ourselves, not our past, and definitely not on the obstacles before us—together Pam and I have enjoyed more than 32 years of marital bliss and raised three (now grown) kids who love and serve Jesus. If you choose to obey God and take Him at His Word, He will be with you step by step. That's a promise! Today, instead of looking at the obstacles look at the One who said, "These things I have spoken to you, so that in Me you may have peace. In the world you have tribulation, but take courage; I have overcome the world" (John 16:33 NASB).

Dear Lord, give us strong hearts for the journey of our lives and remind us that all things are possible with Your presence. Amen.

Deep Roots

*You have planted them, and they have taken
root; they grow and bear fruit.*
JEREMIAH 12:2

If you live in the part of the world known as *Tornado Alley*, you know what happens when a big storm hits. Winds whip through the streets and trees that have shallow roots are tossed about like toothpicks. But trees with deep roots that go far into the ground are anchored in place. These deeply rooted trees continue to grow year after year and survive storm after storm.

God challenges us to have those same kinds of deep roots:

They will be like a tree planted by the water that sends out its roots by the stream. It does not fear when heat comes; its leaves are always green. It has no worries in a year of drought and never fails to bear fruit (Jeremiah 17:8).

Jesus warns of the danger of having shallow roots in the famous parable of the sower:

"Some [seed] fell on rocky places, where it did not have much soil. It sprang up quickly, because the soil was shallow. But when the sun came up, the plants were scorched, and they withered because they had no root" (Mark 4:5-6).

We need more marriages with deep spiritual roots. These strong marriages provide stability for families, churches, and communities. But deep roots take a little effort to develop.

We often have couples say to us, "We want a marriage like yours." Then we begin to explain some of the traditions, habits, and choices that have gone into making a marriage that is truly happy (and, at the writing of this book, successful for 32 wonderful years!). We encourage these couples to have a daily quiet time with God so He can speak to them, teaching them how to be the best partner, parent, and person possible. Then we explain the benefits of layering in good training by attending church, perhaps a Sunday school class, and a small group where couples meet together to study marriage and family issues. We elaborate on the need for marriage conferences and listening to Christian radio, TV, podcasts, and other forms of media so you have a steady intake of God's view of how relationships work.

The response we get about 50 percent of the time is, "Oh, we don't have time for all that!" And our reply is, "You can give time early and prevent issues, or you can give more time later because you *have* issues. You will give time. Pay now or pay later, but you will pay." We just prefer to pay our time in preventing problems and issues.

One young couple came up to us after a conference and said, "We loved the video curriculum!" I (Pam) asked, "So which part of the Bible study did you find most helpful?" The newlywed couple said, "Oh, we didn't do the Bible study. That was too much work. We just watched the video part because you and Bill are funny."

My heart broke for them. While we strive to be practical, biblical, and yes, humorous in our video, we know the real, deep, rich work God does is in those daily Bible studies. Deep roots develop when it is just you and God dealing with your life, your relationship, and your heart. A media-only diet is like a tree with shallow roots. One big windstorm comes and it can topple the tree. Or one hot, scorching summer hits and shallow roots dry up and the plant dies. The best fruit, the sweetest fruit, comes when the roots of the tree go deep down into the rich soil.

We join the apostle Paul as we pray for the marriages of every couple who will read this book:

And I pray that you, being rooted and established in love, may have power, together with all the Lord's holy people, to grasp how wide and long and high and deep is the love of Christ, and to know this love that surpasses knowledge—that you may be filled to the measure of all the fullness of God (Ephesians 3:17-19).

Lord, sink our roots deep into You and Your Word.
Give us the sweet fruit that comes with deep roots
built on the kind of love only You
can give. Amen.

Different from Me

Each one should test their own actions.
GALATIANS 6:4

Every once in a while we encounter reminders that we live in a world of people we don't understand very well. I (Bill) was using the restroom in a restaurant when a young man walked in wearing the biggest earrings I have ever seen. I am not exaggerating when I say they were as big around as a breakfast biscuit. They were not the kind you attach to the ear either. He had obviously spent years diligently stretching his skin because his earlobes were wrapped around the saucers. I didn't mean to engage in an obvious double take but I couldn't help myself.

I tried to hold back but I had to ask. "How long did it take you to be able to wear those?"

He just shrugged and replied, "I don't know. A while, man."

He seemed offended that I took notice, but how could I not? They were huge and seemed to be screaming at me to respond. I wanted to engage him in a longer discussion about his dramatic appearance but it was not the time or place. I left the restaurant thinking, *There are a lot of people in this world who are very different from me.* And then came the unexpected thought, *In fact, I am married to someone who approaches life much differently than I do. How am I supposed to relate to these differences?*

In this regard, Paul gives insightful bullet points in Galatians 6:

• *Restore.* Everyone in the world is insecure, insufficient, and inconsistent, which leads to unfortunate behavior. Therefore, one of life's primary pursuits is to make it easy for one another to get back on track. Live a restorative love: "Brothers and sisters, if someone is caught in a sin, you who live by the Spirit should restore that person gently. But watch yourselves, or you also may be tempted" (verse 1). This restorative love can extend to your spouse too. If he or she fails you, seek to restore him or her so you can both get back on track together quickly.

- *Reach out.* Be compassionate first. We see behavior long before we see the condition of the heart. I was tempted to reach quick conclusions about the man with the earrings because of his outward appearance. It is possible he has a rebellious spirit and will never submit to the authority of Christ. It is just as possible that he has a wounded soul and is crying out to be noticed by others who will love him. It takes a relationship, wisdom, and compassion to know the difference. "Carry each other's burdens, and in this way you will fulfill the law of Christ" (verse 2). Before you jump to conclusions about your mate's choices and behaviors, seek compassion, kindness, and mercy. This way you will be more likely to gain greater understanding into your mate's life and heart.

- *Relax.* Don't be reactionary; live *deliberately.*
  We all tend to decide who we are in reaction to
  others. If other people love us, we are gentle
  and easy to get along with. If other people get
  angry, we fire back or shrink away. If others
  are making bad decisions, we change our
  behavior to either join them in going off track
  or desperately try to manipulate them to turn
  around. When we do this, we empower others
  as we give them control of who we are. The
  healthier approach is to determine who we
  want to be based on how God made us and
  then seek to be that person in all situations. "If
  anyone thinks they are something when they
  are not, they deceive themselves. Each one
  should test their own actions. Then they can
  take pride in themselves alone, without com-
  paring themselves to someone else, for each
  one should carry their own load" (verses 3-5).

If your mate is making unwise choices, instead
of resorting to anger, yelling, manipulation, name-
calling, or a host of other frantic actions, make a list
of the character qualities you want to see in your
own life, and then live those out. As you become

more and more healthy, your mate will be pressured to confront their unwise choices and prayerfully move his or her life in a healthier direction. At the very least, by deciding to live a healthy life you'll keep yourself from getting sucked into the vortex of chaos created by the toxic choices of those around you. In choosing to walk out these three simple steps, you will be living out God's command to test your own actions. Obedience to God will always lead love to a better, stronger, healthier marriage.

Dear Lord, help us see the value in our differences so we can be stronger together. Help each of us look to our own actions and choose health. Amen.

Country Common Sense

*Those who work their land will have
abundant food, but those who chase
fantasies have no sense.*

PROVERBS 12:11

I (Pam) grew up on the farm—a dairy farm, to be exact. My grandparents were married for over 60 years—and for the most part, they were very happy. Their home was the shelter I ran to when my own alcoholic father became brutal or out of control. I learned common sense from Grandma and Grandpa. If Grandpa was frustrated with Grandma, he'd just go to his shop and work, and if my grandmother was irritated with my grandfather, she'd bake, clean, or cook. They didn't waste their anger.

As a counselor once explained to us over dinner, "There are two ways to handle anger: depression and dysfunction, under-achieve or over-achieve. The upside of over-achievement is that you turn the dysfunction into energy and you work hard…so at least you can afford to pay for counseling!"

Bill and I have discovered that uncontrolled anger can lead to lashing out verbally. And then you have a big emotional mess to clean up: arguments, apologies, and meetings that can become very time-consuming. But if we will each do a few things when angry or irritated, our lives will run more smoothly and we will have fewer time-consuming arguments:

Pray. We each ask for God's view of the conflict. We might journal, research the Bible, or simply go for a walk or run and talk to God before we talk more to each other.

Produce. We just keep working on the next healthy thing: our writing, speaking, planning, meetings, etc. By moving our life together forward we are silently saying, "We are in this for the long haul. We are confident God will show us the solution in His time."

Plan to bless. We will each begin to do kind things for each other. Bill might take out the trash without a reminder, or I might bring him a cup of coffee without him needing to request it. Doing kind things softens our hearts so that when we are ready to dialogue, we like each other better.

Prepare the timing. We plan the best time to pick up the discussion. We try to avoid important topics late at night or first thing in the morning, or if the other is preparing for an important speaking engagement, media interview, or meeting, or under a vital pressing deadline. Of course, sometimes we will have to deal with an issue under less than perfect conditions. But if we can, we try to bring our best selves to the table.

Pray together. Before we begin the dialogue and discussion again, we pray and ask God to be in the middle of the conversation.

People ask us how we have written 37 books in our 32 years of marriage while we were also serving in church ministry, raising our children, and serving our communities. Well, you can bet we didn't waste a lot of time or energy arguing inefficiently. Try it!

Next time you are upset, push *pause* on the argument and walk through this simple process. See if it works for the two of you as well as it has for us. The worst outcome will be that you two are productive and you have the funds to pay for your own counselor and the three of you can work with God toward a win-win outcome. Civility and kind speech saves time and increases the chances of success in your marriage.

Lord, help us work through our issues rather than work up more drama. Calm our hearts, and focus them on You and the solutions You will bring.
Amen.

Figuring Out Father

Understand what the Lord's will is.
Ephesians 5:17

A friend recently asked us, "If your father wasn't a good role model, is it hard to figure out how to relate to God as your heavenly Father?" It is such a good question because we all assume God is kind of like our dads. Intellectually, we know that He is perfect, wise, and loving, but our emotions don't always listen to our minds. We spend our most formative years adjusting to our dads, so our impression of what it means to be a father is ingrained in our instincts. If your dad was a solid example, this is good news. Your understanding of God as your heavenly Father will be healthy, dependable, and encouraging. If, however, your dad was unpredictable, severely inconsistent, uninvolved, or simply nonexistent, you have a lot to overcome.

This question was hovering in our minds when we read Ephesians 5:17-20 today. I (Bill) noticed in this passage a number of truths about God as our Dad that I want to hold onto and make instinctive:

- He wants us to find and fulfill our unique contribution to life. "Therefore do not be foolish, but understand what the Lord's will is." God has a will and it includes us. His will is mature, focused, and effective. That is why the opposite of it is referred to as foolishness. God knows who you are and what you were designed for. As a faithful Father, He is working to help you discover your purpose.

- He wants us to be energetic and powerful. "Do not get drunk on wine, which leads to debauchery. Instead, be filled with the Spirit." When someone is under the influence of alcohol, he says things he wouldn't normally say, does things he wouldn't normally do, and has a boldness about him that is not characteristic of his ordinary life. In the same way, the Holy Spirit was put in us by our Father to give us words, actions, and attitudes that can influence others for *good*.

- He wants us to have healthy relationships. The natural result of being under the influence of the Holy Spirit is we speak "to one another with psalms, hymns, and songs from the Spirit." And we will "sing and make music from [our hearts] to the Lord." This doesn't mean we walk around singing all the time and answering everyone with music. It does mean we will naturally encourage others to grow and we will seek to include Jesus in our lives in a daily, natural way.

- He wants us to have a positive, grateful attitude, "...always giving thanks to God the Father for everything, in the name of our Lord Jesus Christ." Zig Ziglar is famous for saying, "A positive attitude will not allow you to do everything. But a positive attitude will allow you to do everything better than a negative attitude will."

Our dads should have equipped us to have all these things in life. Some of you reading this can rejoice because your dad did that for you. Others of you just feel a void. We can all move forward from here, however. And we should, because how we relate to our own fathers, as well as God the Father, will impact the way we relate in relationships. We can build on the good stuff our earthly dads gave us, or we can lean on our heavenly Father to equip us for the future and all the relationships He will send our way. We can learn the truth about God the Father from His Word, and it will help us in our ability to be "Love-Wise." And this way, we can help the next generation get a head start on being "Love-Wise" too.

Lord, give us a clearer understanding
of who You are as a Father so we can live
stronger lives.

Home Is an Attitude

*Yet I am always with you; you hold me by my
right hand. You guide me with your counsel.*
PSALMS 73:23-24

People ask if I (Pam) miss my home because I
travel so much. (I was away from the house 230 days
last year.) But my reply is always, "Home is where
your heart is." My heart is with God, and He says:

"Never will I leave you; never will I forsake you"
(Hebrews 13:5).

"The LORD your God will be with you wherever
you go" (Joshua 1:9).

"You will be blessed when you come in and blessed when you go out" (Deuteronomy 28:6).

My heart is also with Bill, and on most trips he is with me. In addition, my heart is with my kids and grandkids, and we are a far-flung family so our ministry travels actually help us see our family more often. My heart is with the people I love, and we feel so blessed to have friends all over the world. Home is not a house; it is an attitude.

In a world where so many couples "commute to marriage" because of the need to travel for work, military service, or for ministry, it is vital to remember: "Where your treasure is, there your heart will be also" (Matthew 6:21). A study of commuter marriages revealed that "Having a clear set of shared goals and being able to ask for assurance are essential for commuter marriages to work."[5] In other words, feeling that marriage and the family are your treasure, and sensing you are also treasured by your spouse even when away are vital for all marriages, but especially ones with the additional stress of travel or separation by geographical distance. Are you treasuring your relationships more than your house?

Early in our marriage and young family's life, we decided we would look for ways to squeeze out more time together. If that meant packing up a dinner and meeting Bill between ministry meetings at church or bringing some fast food to the football sidelines so we could all capture a few minutes together, we would do that. Even now that our kids are grown, our attitude is "It's worth the hassle for the family to be together." This attitude helps us prioritize flights or drives to our children. Seeing them is more valuable than putting in that new Jacuzzi or remodeling our home. In our marriage mission statement, which we penned as newlyweds, we have a line that reads, "People are more important than material goods." Our treasure is not in making our house beautiful but rather in creating a marriage and a family filled with beautiful, healthy, happy relationships. That is what home means to us.

Jesus modeled this "Home is an attitude" way of life. He once said, "Foxes have dens and birds have nests, but the Son of Man has no place to lay his head" (Matthew 8:20). He had no pillow, but He had friends. He had no recliner to park Himself in, but

He had a close relationship with the Father. He didn't own an abode, but He personified the term *abide*.

It is an admirable goal to create a house that is truly a home, filled with love and all the ingredients that go into making it a cozy, comfortable, and calm atmosphere. A place where you can recharge, renew, and re-energize. As Bill and I have traveled and stayed with many families of all economic levels, we've discovered that it is the "people first" attitude that helps one succeed at making a house a home. The goal is to have a home that is a safe place—not just a showplace. Loosen your grip on your stuff and you will find a new freedom.

One day Bill and I were standing at the check-in counter at the airport when my cell phone rang. It was my assistant. She said, "Pam, my husband (a police officer) drove by your home and the front door was wide open. He checked it out and it looks like all your stuff is still in place, but I don't really know if what matters to you is still there."

I replied, "It isn't," then glanced over to my precious husband standing next to me. I added, "What matters most to me is right here with me."

Lord, help us prioritize people above things. Help us learn how to turn a house into a home. Amen.

Day 14

Honoring Mom

Honor your father and mother—which is the first commandment with a promise—that it may go well with you and that you may enjoy long life on the earth.
EPHESIANS 6:2-3

This year my (Bill's) mom celebrated her eighty-second birthday. Just like you, I have an imperfect mother and I could easily spend time telling you the things I wish had been different about my childhood. Today, however, I simply want to look for a way to honor the legacy I have been given. Honor means to "show respect, give recognition, often implying action to show that honor."[6]

Let me give an example of taking action to give honor. Here are just a few ways that our marriage has been enriched by the woman God chose to be my mom:

- I am grateful she paid the price to give me life. Pam and I have experienced three pregnancies together. All of them have been gloriously uncomfortable, strenuous, and challenging. My mom endured that so I could be here.

- Pam and I are both grateful that my mother faithfully stayed at the task of raising me. We have raised three kids and are intensely aware of the sleepless nights, relentless schedule, demanding need to discipline, and confusing moments of "What do I do next?" that accompany being a parent. My mom persevered through all the challenges I brought her way.

- I am grateful for a legacy of creativity. My mom thinks creatively all the time. It gets funny sometimes, when she tries to connect dots that don't necessarily line up the way she thinks they do, but it is always creative. (Most recently, she explained to us that if our state decided you were a local hero, it would reward you by letting you win the lottery! This is, of course, not true, but my mom described it with vibrancy and enthusiasm.) Much of my mom's creative genius has been buried by fear, but we still see in her an insatiable appetite to entertain new ideas, pursue new solutions, and dream of new adventures.

- I am grateful for her DNA. My mom is still strong and active. She does yard work every day. She walks at a brisk pace. She still does her own housework, maintains a storehouse of food, and explores the Internet. My confidence that I will live a long, active life is high when I look at the energy my mom has after more than eight decades of living.

- I am grateful for a mom who is independent. Again, fear has isolated my mom from many who would have benefited from her gifts, but she established a legacy for me and my siblings that served us well. My siblings and I have all been willing to independently figure out who we are, what we love to do, and what risks we need to take to get there. We have all flown around the world more than the average person. We have all found careers we are willing to put focused effort into. We have all discovered causes we care about that have been worth sacrificing for.

- I am grateful for her commitment to my dad. This year they celebrated their fifty-ninth wedding anniversary. They had significant disagreements over the years but my mom stuck with it. My dad had a serious stroke in his late forties that altered his physical capabilities but my mom refused to give up on their partnership. It has been an imperfect journey but they took the whole trip together.

We can only hope that we improve on their legacy. It is our goal to give to our kids, grandkids, and great-grandkids reasons to be proud that God chose them to be a part of our family.

How can you two take action to show some honor to your parents? Even though Pam and I both come from imperfect, dysfunctional, and sometimes even toxic homes of origin, we have each taken the time to salvage jewels from the ruins and create ways to show honor to our parents. We want to model honor before our own children so that someday they will live in a way that shows honor to us!

Can you take the legacy you have been handed and look at the upside? Look at the things that were right—even if the only one you can think of is "my mom chose life so I could be born." Now make a list of what you want to add to your legacy to benefit the next generation.

Lord, thank You for our family. Help us build a legacy that future generations will be proud of. Amen.

Hot Stuff!

*Take me away with you—let us hurry! Let the
king bring me into his chambers.*
SONG OF SONGS 1:4

We appreciate the heart of the Millers. Nate
was named *Redbook's Hottest Hubby* for 2012.[7] His
wife, Denise, nominated him for his thoughtful-
ness, and the readers agreed—especially when they
heard how he organized his pastor and their friends
to meet them on the top of a mountain where the
Millers were camping and boating with their family. Nate hiked Denise to the top of the knoll to be
greeted by the crowd and he asked her to marry
him all over again. There they held a surprise vow
renewal ceremony.

The Millers are just one example that proves one of the main points we make in our book *Red Hot Monogamy:* The more passionate you are toward God, the more God boomerangs that passion back into your marriage! While researching, we came across a series of statistics that backed up the anecdotal conclusions we had been drawing over our 30 years of working with couples. For example:

The average divorce rate is 50 percent (second marriages end 78 percent of the time, and third-time marriages end 87 percent of the time!), but couples that pray together daily rate their "red-hot monogamy" sex life with five stars. Only one percent of these couples divorce!

Couples that attend church at least weekly rate their sex life with top marks. Couples that have a small group of friends that believe in long-term love (such as one would find in a church marriage small group) rate their love life with high marks as well.

So how do we know God is on our side as a couple? His Word explains that marriage reflects His relationship with the church:

Husbands, love your wives, just as Christ loved the church and gave himself up for her to make her holy, cleansing her by the washing with water through the word, and to present her to himself as a radiant church, without stain or wrinkle or any other blemish, but holy and blameless. In this same way, husbands ought to love their wives as their own bodies. He who loves his wife loves himself. After all, no one ever hated their own body, but they feed and care for their body, just as Christ does the church—for we are members of his body. "For this reason a man will leave his father and mother and be united to his wife, and the two will become one flesh." This is a profound mystery—but I am talking about Christ and the church (Ephesians 5:25-32).

Do you catch this? The way we love our spouse is a reflection of Christ and the church. This is countercultural—exactly the opposite of the trends we see in headlines and media promoting the idea that singles sleeping around are having the most sex or the hottest sex. Television programs like *Sex in the City* (which detailed the sex lives of singles in New

York City) are promoting a myth that the hottest sex is found in serial, noncommittal one-night stands. Really the opposite is true. It is *marriage* which creates a safe setting for love and sex. It is through commitment to your one and only through monogamy that a sex life becomes truly hot. In our book *Red-Hot Monogamy* we continue this train of thought:

Couples that are in long-term, married, monogamous relationships rate their overall sexual satisfaction much higher than their single counterparts. So a statistically accurate portrayal of *Sex in the City* would tell the stories of the love lives of the pastor and his wife or of the other couples sitting in the pews each Sunday. That's where the sizzling sex really is—in the marriages of those who are passionately committed to God and each other! Those are some headlines you don't see every day.

What are you doing to promote trust in your love life? First Corinthians 4:2 suggests the solution: "It is required that those who have been given a trust must prove faithful." If you are dating, waiting until

marriage for sex builds trust because your partner sees your ability to maintain self-control. This
way, he or she knows that later, once you're married,
you'll be able to maintain that same self-control and
say *no* to extramarital affairs. If you are married, you
increase trust with daily small romantic gestures,
prioritizing time with your spouse, and keeping
your word when you promise to be intimate with
your mate. Today be "hot" by being trustworthy.

Lord, help me be trustworthy in the small things so
we can reap the blessing of a red-hot love life in
marriage. Amen.

Humble Choices

Those who humble themselves will be exalted.
LUKE 14:11

He sat in my office, his marriage in ruins, yet he was still pridefully proclaiming all the things his wife needed to do, his kids needed to do, and even what God needed to do. Nothing seemed to be his fault. This man's arrogance was the biggest roadblock to healing his own family.

We can all drift into conceit and smugness unless we are willing to let ourselves be humbled. *To humble* means "to depress" and in Hebrew, the word *humbly* implies a stance of bowing, stooping or crouching as in worship.[8]

Every day we have a choice. We can humbly cooperate with the way life is and bow to trust God, or we can arrogantly try to define life the way we want it to be and attempt to boss God around. In this regard, the ancient nation of Israel is the ultimate example for the rest of us. Whenever they sought to humbly follow God's lead, things went well for them. Their economy flourished, their enemies backed off, their personal well-being improved, and they lived in peace. But whenever they proudly decided that they had the right to devise their own way of living, steps were set in motion to get them to return to humility and faithful living. God sent setbacks to motivate them, then prophets to warn them, and finally calamity to discipline them. Isaiah was one of the prophets who was attempting to get the attention of the nation. In Isaiah 5:18-23, he showed us how to recognize humility by describing what we ought to avoid:

- *The humble accept what is true.* "Woe to those who draw sin along with cords of deceit, and wickedness as with cart ropes" (verse 18). What a graphic picture of a person who has a cart or trailer loaded with deceitful schemes and who is defiantly looking for a way to put them into practice. Rather than dumping the load and replacing it with worthwhile goods, he is defiantly looking for a market for products that will help no one.

- *The humble are patient.* "[Woe] to those who say, 'Let God hurry; let him hasten his work so we may see it'" (verse 19). Many people confuse God's historic patience with inability. They think, *Since He isn't doing it right now, He can't do it.* The humble realize it is never a question of power. It is simply a matter of timing.

- *The humble call good things good.* "Woe to those who call evil good and good evil" (verse 20). This is the age-old argument between God's ways and man's ways. Ever since the fall of mankind, people have loved the darkness and have searched for ways to justify whatever they want to do. Humility says, "I didn't create life so I must accept it the way it is. I don't have the right to redefine life but I do have the privilege of enjoying the good things God has made."

- *The humble are willing to learn.* "Woe to those who are wise in their own eyes and clever in their own sight" (verse 21).

- *The humble love sobriety and self-control.* "Woe to those who are heroes at drinking wine and champions at mixing drinks" (verse 22).

It seems almost too simple to be a problem. If you were to ask people, "Do you want to do what is true, be a patient person, love what is good, be willing to learn, and possess self-control?" you would expect most people to say *yes.* In action, however, most of us have done the opposite. Today we need to choose to be humble. Today we need to be determined to wait on God. Today we need to be willing to learn. Today we need to bow to God's will and God's ways.

Dear God, give us Your strength today to humbly accept life the way You created it. Amen.

I Am Going to Out-Love You!

"My food," said Jesus, "is to do the will of him who sent me and to finish his work."

Jesus was a good son. Bill and I have three good sons, so we recognize one when we see one! A good son carries out the will of his father. A good son represents his family well and moves the family legacy forward. Good daughters would do the same. These are people who value the heritage that has been handed to them. They know how to build upon that strong foundation.

Within minutes of meeting John and Barb Schaller, we knew they shared a special and unusual love. Barb found it easy to gush about how blessed and fortunate she found it to be married to John. John found it easy to compliment a wife who he was obviously endeared to, judging by the gleam in his eyes! They are our peers in marriage, married about the same amount of time as Bill and me (over three decades!). When I asked Barb the secret of their long-lasting love, she said, "My husband forgives easily. He is full of grace, mercy, and forgiveness." When we asked John the same question, his reply was similar: "My wife knows how to keep giving love when people are hard to love. She loves unconditionally and tenaciously." Do you notice how these responses are really just two sides of the same coin? He loves without limits and she is limitless in her love.

They are the owners of Morning Star Dairy. They still live in the home John was raised in. John is the youngest of twelve children, so he had the good fortune to watch his parents enjoy a lifelong love. Love is a rich heritage on Morning Star farm. John describes his mother as a saint who loved lavishly, never uttered a harsh word, and possessed a servant's heart. Her heart of love was often expressed toward her husband as she darted about the kitchen, waiting on him with an affectionate, "On the way, Daddy baby!" And that legacy of love continues. One will sometimes hear Barb call John *Daddy,* and with a twinkle in his eye and a sheepish grin he will tease back, "That's Daddy *baby* to you."

How does one go about building a legacy of love that passes from generation to generation? Follow John and Barb's pattern and put their example into action: simply *out-love* and *out-serve* one another. Love is an action verb, and it is best expressed with a servant's attitude. What is a servant's attitude? Philippians 2:3-7 captures it best when the apostle Paul simply says:

Do nothing out of selfish ambition or vain conceit. Rather, in humility value others above yourselves, not looking to your own interests but each of you to the interests of the others. In your relationships with one another, have the same mindset as Christ Jesus: Who, being in very nature God, did not consider equality with God something to be used to his own advantage; rather, he made himself nothing by taking the very nature of a servant.

Today, ask God to help you cultivate a "you first" attitude and seek to place your mate's needs as a priority on your heart. The plus side of having a servant's attitude is your children are watching, and perhaps you will be laying the foundation of a family in which everyone seeks to out-love the other!

Lord, help me not seek my own interests as the first priority but help me look out for my mate's needs. Give me Your same heart and attitude, Jesus. Help us to lay a legacy of love. Amen.

I Can't Believe I Said That

*The tongue is a small part of the body,
but it makes great boasts.*
JAMES 3:5

I was having a great time with Pam yesterday. We were laughing and getting caught up with one another as we shared stories of the week. Then, for some unknown reason, I blurted out a comment that was just really insensitive. It was one of those moments in life when you realize just a little too late that what you are saying is not going to accomplish anything good. I was stunned at myself. I wasn't trying to be mean and hadn't intended to cause her pain. But my words were mean, thoughtless, and could easily be interpreted as hurtful. There are times, to be sure, when my attitude is childish and I say things with a little bite in my tongue…but this wasn't one of them. I was enjoying Pam's company and I wasn't aware of anything that was bugging me. It really was a slip of the tongue, and I could tell Pam was surprised that words so cutting had rolled out of my mouth. It was uncharacteristic and her wide eyes of shock revealed my error.

Without hesitation, I followed up the insensitive announcement with, "I can't believe I just said that. That was so insensitive. I obviously wasn't thinking because I would never have planned to say what I just said."

I looked at Pam to see how she was doing and I could tell she was still a little stunned, so I kept talking. "Really, Pam, I can't believe I just said that. I don't even believe the words that came out of my mouth. That was so weird. I didn't even have time to reel them back in, they just blurted out like they had a mind of their own. Whoa, that was really insensitive."

Fortunately, my rambling rescued the mood. Pam gave me the benefit of the doubt. What could have been a hurtful, lingering memory got us both laughing. Pam extended grace because I have a long enough track record of sensitivity toward her, and she accepts the principle that the tongue has a mind of its own and gets carried away sometimes.

It was a perfect example for us of James 3:2-10:

We all stumble in many ways. Anyone who is never at fault in what they say is perfect, able to keep their whole body in check…the tongue is a small part of the body, but it makes great boasts. Consider what a great forest is set on fire by a small spark. The tongue also is a fire…It corrupts the whole body, sets the whole course of one's life on fire, and is itself set on fire by hell…With the tongue we praise our Lord and Father, and with it we curse human beings, who have been made in God's likeness. Out of the same mouth come praise and cursing. My brothers and sisters, this should not be.

So what exactly did I say to Pam that was so insensitive? Well, it wasn't a good thing to say the first time and I am not foolish enough to repeat it here. You will just have to imagine what it might have been based on your own experience. Today, pause a moment before you blurt away. Write down your words before you lash out. Or if you have a habit of putting your foot in your mouth, record yourself speaking. Later, listen to the recording and ask yourself how you might change your words to better reflect how God would talk to your mate, your family, your friends, and your coworkers.

Lord, give us a soft heart so we say encouraging things to one another. Help us recover quickly when the wrong words blurt out. Amen.

In the Pressure Cooker

You know that under pressure, your faith-life is forced into the open and shows its true colors.
JAMES 1:3 MSG

I (Pam) grew up on a farm and canning vegetables was just part of our lifestyle. To accomplish this, we often used a pressure cooker. So how does a pressure cooker work? Online kitchen expert Miss Vickie describes it like this:

The only way to make the steam hotter (and/or to boil the water at a higher temperature) is to put the system under pressure. This is what a pressure cooker does. If we fit an absolutely tight cover to the pan so no steam can escape while we continue to add heat, both the pressure and temperature inside the vessel will rise…Steam has six times the heat potential…This increased heat transfer potential is why steam is such an effective cooking medium.[9]

Pressure can make your marriage better too. Just as food in a pressure cooker will be preserved well and taste scrumptious, so will your marriage become "tastier" if it can handle the pressure.

In the book *10 Secrets to Living Smart, Savvy and Strong*, I share in detail one of the pressure-cooker times of our marriage: Bill was ill, all three of our sons had been injured playing football, my brother had a heart attack, and I felt torn with the painful question of "Who do I help first?" In addition, finances were exceptionally tight and we were dealing with an emotionally painful conflict with people we trusted. And that's not even mentioning the daily pressures of midlife: hot flashes, night sweats, and the aches and pains of aging bodies and minds.

The apostle Paul knew all about this kind of stress: "We are hard pressed on every side, but not crushed; perplexed, but not in despair; persecuted, but not abandoned; struck down, but not destroyed" (2 Corinthians 4:8-9).

Hard pressed means *to press upon*, like in a vise; perplexed is a term for puzzled; persecuted is the picture of harassing to cause pain; and struck down is the knockout punch but not a death blow. Do you ever feel like you and your mate are there? Are you pressed in from every side, puzzled, harassed, and knocked to the ground by life?

In those times, it is easy to play the blame game. *If he would have only done this*, or *She should have known to do that*. This is a no-win spiral down that slippery slope. That is like opening up the pressure cooker too early—which can cause a big mess!

If you've ever heard of a pressure cooker exploding, the most likely cause was that the cooker was forced open before it had completely cooled down. When the cooker is opened too early, it can "blow a gasket" and the pressurized contents will explode all over! You can best avoid a blowup by waiting until the pressure has dropped before opening the lid. It's the same with your marriage.

In *The 10 Best Decisions a Couple Can Make*, we share how we try to handle life in the pressure cooker. Instead of blaming each other—which only adds steam into the cooker and may cause one or both of you to "blow a gasket"—follow our example instead! We safely defuse the pressure by looking at each other and saying, "It's not you; it's not me; it's just *life!*"

Lord, help us not blame one another. Instead help us safely release steam for each other when we're caught in the pressure cooker of life. Amen.

Instrument or Ornament?

Do not offer any part of yourself to sin as an instrument of wickedness, but rather offer yourselves to God as those who have been brought from death to life; and offer every part of yourself to him as an instrument of righteousness.

ROMANS 6:13

Don and Darla listened intently as their pastor, Steve Larson, shared the title of his sermon "Instrument or Ornament?" The concept is an easy one to assimilate but much harder to live out. Basically, we all have loves, passions, and material goods that can become a showcase for our own glory or our own enjoyment. These are the *ornaments* that adorn our lives. But God has a higher calling for us—one that turns an ornament into an instrument. We are called to hold our possessions and even our own lives with an open palm. God is asking you to lift up your treasures, your time, and your talent for His use, to further His agenda.

Don and Darla applied their pastor's good advice. They coordinated a car show, featuring Don's prized restored Corvette, and held it after a Sunday morning worship service to pique men's interest in attending church.

In our ministry, we see a trail of people who took care to use their lives and possessions as instruments for furthering God's work. Jerry and Lane opened up their backyard—complete with pool and barbeque—for the church's youth group. Marion and Brian opened up their home and their beautiful backyard for many of our Love-Wise events. Jack and Robin, Mark and Maria, and Steve and Penny all opened up their homes for weekly Bible studies. Rose and Dan loaned the jet skis for a father and son trip. Rob and Melinda owned the most exclusive dress boutique in town, yet clothed Pam as we headed to seminary. Bill and Nora saw our need for a car to complete our seminary degree, so they put up part of the funding. Bill and Janeen gave us a refrigerator so we could move into a nicer but lower-rent apartment. Barbara and Tom let us live with them rent-free for four months so we could save for seminary. And we could name *many* more people on our journey whom God has used to build us, our family, and the ministry He entrusted to us. If these brave couples had not been willing to open up their lives for God's use, this book might not be in your hands.

All that we are and all that we own is really God's. He has trusted it to our care—but for His use:

Yours, LORD, is the greatness and the power
and the glory and the majesty and the splendor,
for everything in heaven and earth is yours.
Yours, LORD, is the kingdom;
you are exalted as head over all.
Wealth and honor come from you;
you are the ruler of all things.

In your hands are strength and power
  to exalt and give strength to all
(1 Chronicles 29:11-12).

What about the two of you? Do you own a home, a car, a boat, or anything else you think God could use to bring people to Himself? Each Christmas when we were pastoring, people volunteered their talents to host small parties in their homes. I remember women sharing skills like cake baking, flower arranging, decorating, and a myriad of other talents to interest the unchurched in coming to a gathering of friends where they might hear about the love of Christ and how God offers His friendship to us. And for years, the guys threw "Turkeybowl" father-son football games and a Super Bowl party outreach. They shared our family love of football in such a way that men could also learn how to embrace Jesus for the real power in this life.

Look around you right now. What in your surroundings might you offer up as an instrument of God's service?

Lord, let us be generous with all You have given
to us: our time, our talents, our treasures. We offer
all we are and all we have to You for Your use,
because it was You who first entrusted it to us.
Amen.

Irritating Strengths

Ask where the good way is, and walk in it.
JEREMIAH 6:16

Personal growth is exciting to watch. Just this week, we encountered a couple who was facing a choice: They could either accept that change was necessary and develop new skills in their lives, or they could ignore the call to grow and continue in their familiar discomfort.

This couple has been frustrated for a while because they seem to be in continual friction with each another. They love each other, but their life together seems harder than it should be. He has a relaxed, easygoing, take-it-as-it-comes approach to life. This attitude used to be really attractive to her because she felt calmer when she was around him. She has a sensitive, compassionate approach to life, which he used to find attractive because he felt more important when he was around her. They thought it would be like this forever…but they forgot to factor in responsibility.

Now that they have two kids and active careers, the characteristics they used to love about each other have become irritating. She cares deeply for their children and gets intensely focused on the tasks that need to be completed to support their lives. He, on the other hand, is acutely aware of the constant stress in their lives and senses the need to take time off, look for ways to play, and put the focus on the people themselves rather than all the tasks that take time away from the relationships. They both feel so strongly about their perspective that their strengths have become a platform for conflict.

It is scenarios just like this that make or break our lives. If this couple continues in this trend, it is easy to see that they will grow discouraged and discontent. On the other hand, if they can rediscover that what they love about each other has now become an irritation, they can find a way to reignite the passion of their relationship. They can begin to rely on each other's best traits once again, building a stronger life together than they could ever accomplish as individuals. It will take some work to recapture this perspective but once they find it, life will seem easier to them.

We got to thinking about this couple when we were reading Jeremiah 6:16 during our devotions this morning. "This is what the LORD says: 'Stand at the crossroads and look; ask for the ancient paths, ask where the good way is, and walk in it, and you will find rest for your souls.'" There is always a way to walk that provides rest for our souls. Not because life got any easier, but because we are cooperating with the way God made us and made life.

As we talked about the unique way God made this couple, they had one of those *Aha!* moments. She said, "My husband is so laid-back that I stopped trusting him to make decisions. I just took over and started doing whatever needed to be done. In reaction, he has become more relaxed and almost passive."

He said, "I saw her becoming so frantic about our life that I knew I had to back way off or we would both create so much stress that it would be harmful to our kids."

Together they agreed, "This week we are going to start asking each other, 'Who is the best person to make this decision?' and then trust the other to lead in the areas of their strengths. We honestly believe that will be better for us than what we have been doing."

We are sure the new thinking will lead them down a better path for their life and love because their new method reflects one simple, summary phrase in a familiar marriage passage from the Bible: "Be subject to one another in the fear of Christ" (Ephesians 5:21 NASB).

Jesus, remind us today of the traits we love about each other and how those differences can be used for us and our family. Amen.

Day 22

Kuleana

We proclaim to you what we have seen and heard, so that you also may have fellowship with us. And our fellowship is with the Father and with his Son, Jesus Christ.

1 JOHN 1:3

In the Hawaiian language the term *kuleana* refers to those people you are responsible to and responsible for. It is your accountability system, or, as we like to call it, your success net. If you picture yourself walking the tightrope of life, your *kuleana* are the people who are carrying the net under your life in case you fall. They include family who really know you, friends who walk beside you, your children, your grandchildren, and anyone who looks up to you. Also included are any mentors or leaders who have poured into you. And it definitely includes your spouse.

A smart couple will have a large *kuleana* with whom they can be real, honest, and authentic. Some call it an accountability system. Although the Bible never uses the exact word "accountability," there are plenty of other words that let us know God thinks accountability is vital:

Fellowship or *koinonia*: an association based upon a common bond with willing participation and sharing. True fellowship involves authenticity, which incorporates two key concepts:

Exhortation: called alongside to bring out the best in one another.

Admonish: to put in mind; putting the right thoughts into the minds of others

So it seems God wants us all to have a group—a fellowship—of people we walk alongside, and who walk alongside us. And while we are journeying together, we are to put the right thoughts into each other's minds.

Many people ask Bill and me, "What is the strength of your relationship?" We have to say we are *kuleana* to each other first. We honestly share when we are struggling with something. Too many people keep hidden sins, negative thoughts, and unresolved feelings from their spouse—sometimes even with good intentions, thinking, "I don't want to hurt him or her." While we always think it is wise to talk to God first, and then whomever God directs you to seek counsel from, your mate will often be one of the best people to use as a sounding board in a struggle. He or she knows you best, after all.

Bill and I are responsible to each other in so many areas: how we spend (or save) money, how often we exercise, what we watch on TV or listen to or read, how we raise our children, and all our spiritual disciplines. We are responsible to each other in prayer, Bible study, using our gifts, worship, and yes, the *koinonia* or *kuleana* of building a success net together. Because we talk honestly about what God is teaching us, what the Holy Spirit is convicting us to do and say, and how God wants us to live to better reflect His glory, we are drawn to each other like magnets.

When we were dating, our entire *kuleana* or *koinonia* friendship circle would greet each other with, "Hi! How are you? What's God been teaching you?" Just asking that question was true *kuleana*. We were responsible for learning something from God daily so we'd have an answer to the question! Bill and I continue this habit in our own private spiritual lives.

So today, take a walk with your mate or sit down for some Kona coffee and ask, "So what's God been teaching you?" Enjoy some *kuleana*.

Lord, let our marriage be one of unity, honesty, and authenticity. Give us *koinonia* fellowship that will make each of us better because we are in relationship with each other and with You. Amen.

Day 23

Lost in Translation

*Let us not love with words or speech but with
actions and in truth.*
1 JOHN 3:18

We have a goal to visit the countries that represent the 12 languages our book *Men Are Like Waffles—Women Are Like Spaghetti* has been translated into. Because of our desire to cross cultures, we have often been accompanied by translators. They take what we are saying and reword our thoughts and intentions so that a clear message is presented. To do this, they don't always translate word for word. They adapt our words into the language's speech patterns and idioms, carrying the main concept so the listener gains the heart or meat of the message.

Wouldn't it be nice if we could each have a marital translator? Someone who steps in when we are misunderstanding each other? Good news: The Holy Spirit can be that translator! No one knows your mate like God, so the whisper of the Spirit can help you look past the misstatement or the poorly worded sentence into the heart and intent of your spouse.

Love gives the benefit of the doubt. The apostle Paul puts it this way in Philippians 1:7: "It is right for me to feel this way about all of you, since I have you in my heart." *In my heart* means you carry the person inside in a way that is open-minded. When the apostle Paul wrote this he was complimenting his friends. As one Bible commentary puts it, "It did not matter whether Paul was under arrest…or free; his friends at Philippi shared with him in what God was doing through him…Paul praised them for their concern."[10]

That is a good place to be in a marriage. When you carry each other on your heart, you assume the best about the other person and his or her words. But when you quit carrying your mate on your heart, it becomes all about behavior. The problem with a behavior-based relationship is that no one can behave well enough for long enough to keep a relationship going just on perfect behavior. It is much better to carry your mate on your heart, giving him or her the benefit of the doubt, believing they too want the best for your love.

Next time your feelings are hurt over specific words, go a little deeper and look to the heart of your spouse. Assume he or she is concerned for your best interest. What does he or she have on his or her heart concerning you? If your mate has a history of loving you, assume he or she is trying to love you underneath the fumble with the sentence.

Lord, let us look at the heart history of each other when we are discussing hard things. Let us give each other grace in the moment while we look to reword in a way that matches our heart intent. Help me carry my mate on my heart. Amen.

Where Love and Peace Meet

Love and faithfulness meet together;
righteousness and peace kiss each other.
PSALM 85:10

On the wall of our bedroom is a beautiful portrait taken by a well-known photographer. The photo is black and white, but it was recolored to highlight certain aspects of the portrait. The picture is of Bill and me. In the photo you can't see our faces because I am wearing a hat, but you can tell it was a kiss of love. How?

In the photo I am standing on my tiptoes,

reaching up to give Bill a kiss. That peck was apparently so amazing that it caused Bill to rock back on his heels! (I think this might be where the term "head over heels in love" came from!) The look of our feet in this position of a public display of affection was the selling point, and this photo became the front cover of a *Focus on the Family* book on marriage.

It is imperative to cultivate these kinds of meet-ups of hearts and lives:

- a glance across the room

- the touch of your hand on your mate's

- a small caress

- a squeeze of hands, or footsies under the table

Small touches of affection add up in big ways over time!

When I had the photograph framed, today's verse seemed so appropriate: "Love and faithfulness meet together; righteousness and peace kiss each other." The linking and balance of each couplet is what it takes to have long-lasting love:

Love *and* faithfulness: The passion of love ignites the flame of intimacy, but it is the commitment to faithfulness and fidelity that *keeps* passion alive year after year. When we wrote the book *Red-Hot Monogamy*, we found research showing that trust is the number-one key to unlock passion so a woman can climax during sex. Trust is built with a secure knowledge that your mate is faithful!

Righteousness *and* peace: In marriage, it is important to do things right. Skills like communication, kindness, and servanthood are just a few of the building blocks for love. Sometimes well-meaning spouses fall into the no-win trap of pointing out all the "improvements" the other can make in the relationship. It is easy for the other person to perceive this stance as he or she always needing to be "right." Pushing for what you think is right is not always right! This is where peace comes in. Sometimes we each need to be more accommodating in order to bring peace into the relationship. For example, one day my friend caught herself correcting the way her husband buttered his bread. Now in the scope of all the things that are important in this world the way her man butters bread is miniscule—and she wisely recognized that. That is peacekeeping.

Give grace over voicing your preferences, and save your opinions for the things that truly reflect righteousness: keeping a promise, living with integrity, or committing to love your mate as God loves him or her.

Lord, please help me keep love in balance.
Let love and faithfulness meet in our marriage and
let righteousness and peace kiss. Help
me show my love today in a small gesture of
affection. Amen.

Good Morning

Satisfy us in the morning with your
unfailing love, that we may sing for joy
and be glad all our days.
PSALM 90:14

I love my alarm clock. I know, who says that? But I do, because I have the best alarm clock in the world. In fact, morning is my favorite time of day just because of the relationship I have with my alarm clock! You guessed it—Bill is my alarm! Almost every morning, he gently kisses the nape of my neck and whispers, "Good morning, beautiful. It's time." You might be thinking, "Time for what?" Yes, sometimes intimacy follows the sweet wake-up call, but usually "red-hot monogamy" has to wait until later due to the pressing responsibilities of the day. However, my response back is typically a passionate good-morning kiss for my man, and that sets us up for a better chance at a rendezvous later!

Our day always starts better and usually stays so much better because of that good-morning kiss. Any kind of good-morning greeting is a powerful tool for marital bliss. *Women's Health* printed the results of a commonsense study revealing that women who said "Good morning" to their spouse as they greeted the day actually had better days than those who didn't. In fact, 94 percent of couples who say "Good morning" to each other rate their relationship as excellent.[11]

Morning is important to God too. There are over 1,000 references to the morning in the Bible, including Psalm 65:8: "The whole earth is filled with awe at your wonders; where morning dawns, where evening fades, you call forth songs of joy." God ushers in each sunrise and give stage directions to the party going on in heaven that creates our morning!

Bill and I have a collection of photographs on our computers of sunrises and sunsets. Whenever we have a chance during our travels, we both appreciate the opportunity to take advantage of some sunrises! There is just something hopeful, something joy-filled in embracing the sight of the sun peaking over a mountain, over the water, over a meadow, or over the skyscraper-filled vista. Do an Internet search for the time of sunrise, and plan today to wake each other tomorrow with a kiss and a sunrise. One of you can be the "alarm clock," and the other will respond with a greeting of love. Then head outside to take in God's beautiful party at dawn as He greets you with the love declared in the sunrise.

Lord, help us greet each other with the same kind of delight You give in greeting us each morning.
Amen.

Motivated to Live

He urged them to plead for mercy from
the God of heaven.
DANIEL 2:18

Daniel was having one of those incredibly stressful days. The king had had a troubling dream, and he was going to put all his wise counselors to death unless one of them could explain it to him. If Daniel couldn't interpret the dream, his life would be on the line.

After he got this news, "Daniel returned to his house and explained the matter to his friends Hananiah, Mishael and Azariah. He urged them to plead for mercy from the God of heaven concerning this mystery, so that he and his friends might not be executed with the rest of the wise men of Babylon" (Daniel 2:17-18). These verses got us thinking. We would be highly motivated to pray if we believed execution was imminent! Daniel didn't have to give much explanation or work very hard to persuade his friends to pray—personal survival was a sufficient motivation.

Fortunately, we are not currently living in imminent danger. Still, this scenario led us to ask what motivates *us*. What keeps us committed and provides energy for our pursuits in the midst of the ups and downs of real life? It is impossible to sum up personal motivation in a few simple statements, but we are aware that the following conclusions help keep us going:

We live in partnership with God. After God revealed the king's dream to Daniel, he prayed, "I thank and praise you, God of my ancestors: You have given me wisdom and power, you have made known to me what we asked of you, you have made known to us the dream of the king" (verse 23). Daniel was going to appear before the king, but *God* provided the information he needed to succeed. In a similar fashion, we have work to do, a family to support, responsibilities to pursue, and causes to fight for. Along the way, God provides wisdom and power so that these activities have eternal influence.

We love the people God has put in our life. Just as Daniel had his three friends, God has filled our life with individuals we care deeply about. Our kids, grandkids, and friends are extremely important to us—and each other, of course! We are not always happy with each other or our families and friends, but we always want what is best for them. If we are honest, the times we are upset with them are caused by the sense that they are either underachieving or performing below their abilities. In contrast, we find great satisfaction when anyone in our family learns new things, grows wiser, and develops new skills.

We love helping others succeed. We find great satisfaction in helping others find new insight, persevere in tough circumstances, develop healthier relationships, or discover the skills they need for their personal or professional lives.

We remember the change. There was a time in our lives when we didn't know Jesus and had no sense of what our lives were all about. We did things in life because we enjoyed them or received attention from them. They made us feel important, loved, power-ful, or any one of many misdirected motives. We had no sense that we were created for a purpose. We grew up in dramatic homes and we developed defensive responses to the chaos. But since we met our Savior, the emotional triggers have gradually been replaced with the understanding that "we are God's handiwork, created in Christ Jesus to do good works, which God prepared in advance for us to do" (Ephesians 2:10).

Daniel pled for mercy from God, and God eventually saved him—and then elevated him! His example is a good one to follow. If you don't know where to begin in moving your life or love forward, you can pray a simple prayer. Just cry out, "Lord, have mercy!" You're in good company when you pray that prayer:

As Jesus went on from there, two blind men fol-lowed Him, crying out, "Have mercy on us, Son of David!" (Matthew 9:27 NASB).

When they came to the crowd, a man came up to Jesus, falling on his knees before Him and saying, "Lord, have mercy on my son, for he is a lunatic and is very ill; for he often falls into the fire and often into the water" (Matthew 17:14-15 NASB).

Then they came to Jericho. And as He was leaving Jericho with His disciples and a large crowd, a blind beggar named Bartimaeus, the son of Timaeus, was sitting by the road. When he heard that it was Jesus the Nazarene, he began to cry out and say, "Jesus, Son of David, have mercy on me!" Many were sternly telling him to be quiet, but he kept crying out all the more, "Son of David, have mercy on me!" (Mark 10:46-48 NASB).

Jesus answered each of these cries for mercy—and He will answer your cry. Have mercy!

Jesus, give us confidence as a couple so our obstacles can become opportunities and our setbacks can become successes. We plead Your mercy! Amen.

Day 27

Our Provider

He provides food for those who fear him; he
remembers his covenant forever.
PSALM 111:5

One of the prayers I (Pam) often pray is *Lord, we look to You for Your power, protection, and provision.* I know we can ask this because God offers His character to back up His promises.

In my book *Becoming a Brave New Woman*, I reflect upon God as our Provider:

My favorite name of God is *Jehovah Jireh,* meaning "the one who provides." *Jireh* is the Hebrew verb for *to see.* And if God sees, He also *foresees.* "As the One who possesses eternal wisdom and knowledge, He knows the end from the beginning. As Elohim He is all-knowing, all-wise, and all-powerful. From eternity to eternity He foresees everything. But another word for seeing is vision, from the Latin word *video*—to see."[12] So it's like God has the video for your life! Not only does He have the video, He is the director!

Your opportunities in life directly reflect how you view God. If you know Him, you will trust Him. If you trust Him, you will step out in faith and gain that big wonderful life He promises. A.W. Tozer says in his classic book *The Knowledge of the Holy,* "What comes into our minds when we think about God is the most important thing about us."[13] Henry Blackaby and Claude King agree. In *Experiencing God,* they write, "How you live your life daily is a testimony of what you believe about God."[14] I like to say, "Show me your God, and I will show you your ability to achieve. Small God—small life. Big God—big opportunities and potential await."[15]

There are many times when we as a couple have stepped out on a promise from God, trusting Him to be exactly who He promises He is. Today, let's look at just one area: God as the *Provider*. Bill and I trusted God would provide…

- when we married at age 20 with only part-time jobs and no college diploma.

- when Bill quit his job and we lived on just Pam's salary so Bill could finish two years of college in just one very packed academic year.

- when we went without a car for almost that entire year, riding our bikes and trusting God would somehow provide one. (He did—even though we only had $100 to pay for it!)

- when we set off for Talbot Seminary and Biola University to get training for ministry.

- when we started a family on a youth pastor's salary.

- when we decided Pam would be a stay-at-home mom when our kids were preschoolers.

- when we bought our first home.

- when we remodeled that home.

- when we took a cut in pay for Bill to take a senior pastor position at age 28.

- when our only car died just before the move to San Diego and we only had a few hundred dollars to put toward a new one.

- when we bought property and built a home in San Diego.

- when we stepped out in faith and Pam went back to school to complete her degree.

- when we started our writing and speaking ministry.

Each one of those decisions to trust God helped to lay the foundation for all we are doing today.

God has never let us down. We married young and followed hard after God to complete our education and go to seminary, all while working with youth. And God treated us as His kids. He sent groceries when our cupboards were bare. He sent a car for under $100 after we'd spent a year riding our bikes everywhere we needed to go. He sent supportive families to contribute toward our seminary education because they were thankful we'd shepherded their teens. He sent wise mentors to help us think through the buying of our home, and faithful families who jumped in and helped build another home when we moved into the senior pastorate. God provided for us every step of the way in ways both small and large. We worked hard, yes, very hard. But when our work fell short in providing for our needs, He moved circumstances and the hearts of people to pull off many answers to prayer that we see as pretty miraculous. And He will do that for you. There is just one condition: walk uprightly.

For the Lord God is a sun and shield; the Lord gives grace and glory; no good thing does He withhold from those who walk uprightly (Psalm 84:11 NASB).

Upright means you will be morally good, blameless, genuine, and sincere. Pam's mom used to say, "Live in such a way that you can stand tall." Today, choose to live life so that you can be proud of your choices!

Lord, help us walk full and upright so we can live a life full of Your presence and blessings. Amen.

Patient Promises

Be careful, keep calm and don't be afraid.
ISAIAH 7:4

We are very glad that God's promises are stronger than our attitudes. Even though we know God is faithful, loving, always true, totally committed, righteous, and unchanging, we still grumble, resist, and act foolishly at times. We couldn't help but relate to King Ahaz in Isaiah 7. While Ahaz was the king of Judah, he came under attack. Two kings north of him joined forces and conspired to overthrow him. The threat must have seemed credible because "the hearts of Ahaz and his people were shaken, as the trees of the forest are shaken by the wind" (verse 2). But God was in control of the whole situation. God sent Isaiah to Ahaz to proclaim, "Be careful, keep calm and don't be afraid. Do not lose heart because of these two smoldering stubs of firewood" (verse 4).

God promised to protect, guide, and provide for Ahaz despite the fact that his enemies were fiercely opposed to him. The enemies were plotting his ruin and planning to tear Judah apart (verses 5-6). But as Isaiah reminded the king, despite his enemies' evil intentions everything in Ahaz's life still had to pass through the filter of God's oversight.

> Yet this is what the Sovereign LORD says:
> "It will not take place,
> it will not happen…
> If you do not stand firm in your faith,
> you will not stand at all" (verses 7,9).

To convince Ahaz of His protection, God told him to, "Ask the LORD your God for a sign, whether in the deepest depths or in the highest heights" (verse 11). Now, normally, asking God for a sign is not a good idea since it smacks of manipulation. In this case, however, God initiated the idea so it became a step of obedience. But look how King

Ahaz responded: "I will not ask; I will not put the LORD to the test" (verse 12).

You can almost see God rolling His eyes as Ahaz says this. Telling God that He didn't mean what He said is never a good idea. Isaiah said to the king, "Is it not enough to try the patience of humans? Will you try the patience of my God also? Therefore the Lord himself will give you a sign: The virgin will conceive and give birth to a son, and will call him Immanuel" (verses 13-14).

God is disappointed in Ahaz's attitude and actions. You can sense His frustration as a limited human being tries to outthink an infinite God. And yet in the midst of the mismatch, God makes one of the most important promises in history. The Savior of the world is coming and He can be recognized without a doubt, because He will be born to a virgin.

That is the way our God is. He makes promises because of who He is, not because of who we are.

Each of us can remember a time when God was faithful in spite of our bad attitudes. Here are a few of ours (these aren't the only ones, but these are the ones we're willing to share and 'fess up to!):

When God asked us to go to seminary, I (Pam) was a Negative Nelly at first. I wanted to skip the whole getting a Masters thing and just jump in, buy a home, and have a baby. And I especially didn't want to move to Los Angeles to go to school! Oh— and did I mention that to save money to get there we decided not to buy a car but to ride bikes until God provided a car we could afford? (Our budget? One hundred dollars!) I couldn't believe that I, a former homecoming queen, had to pedal to work! But despite my less than stellar attitude, I learned to love being in the fresh air, praying and praising God. God had to take me kicking and screaming to Los Angeles to attend Biola while Bill attended Talbot Seminary, but those became some of our most precious marriage memories. The relationships we forged there with faculty and friends are still some of the strongest we have today.

Bill's attitude was also challenged when God asked him to move from a desk job as a draftsman at a nice firm with a nice office to work in and go to work in the cold, dirty oil fields to save up money so he could return to college full time. The pay was great but the daily surroundings definitely had him out of his comfort zone.

To pull through these darker days, we each had to decide to thank God for being our Provider. We had to trust that He saw the big picture of our life. Our goals were lofty and we had to pay some high prices to achieve them. God knew we would need to develop character along the path. That was the only way we would be successful once He had placed us in positions of leadership and influence.

He keeps His promises because it is in His nature to do so, not because we have earned what He has offered. He is patient with His promises because He knows they will all be fulfilled—and amazingly, we are the beneficiaries. Need an attitude adjustment? Look to your faithful God.

Jesus, thank You for always doing Your will despite our shortcomings. Help us to keep our focus on Your promises today. Amen.

Perspective on the Journey

*But God stepped in and saved me from
certain death. I'm alive again!
Once more I see the light!*
JOB 33:28 MSG

On one trip home from Asia, our plane was rerouted. We were supposed to come home to California in the early afternoon to spend time with our youngest son (then a senior in high school) before heading out to Chicago the next day. All flights to the entire western side of the USA were filled so they rerouted us to Chicago! It was 80 degrees in Singapore when we departed Asia and a blizzard when we landed in Chicago. We caught the next flight home to San Diego and were there just long enough to sleep a few hours, have breakfast with our son, repack, and allow Bill to keep an important appointment. Then off we went again, and in less than 20 hours we were back in Chicago.

That blizzard was still blowing full-force. It was around midnight when we finally got to the rental car, and we still had a two-hour drive ahead of us to South Bend, Indiana. I noticed that there wasn't a scraper or snow brush in the rental car, so I shuffled back through the snow banks to the rental company to get one.

The radio was announcing road closures. Only the interstate we were on was currently remaining open—but we had no idea for how long! We had a 7:00 a.m. radio interview scheduled at the hotel and an 8:00 a.m. call time for a live in-studio TV appearance. Obligation propelled us forward. Or perhaps it was jet lag—the bed waiting in the hotel tempted us to keep moving! The freeway seemed clear and safe so we moved forward, crawling at a snail's pace.

Just outside Gary, Indiana, a car just in front of us slid on the ice, lost control, and crashed head-on into a tractor trailer. We arrived on the scene at the same time as all the emergency vehicles. We looked to see if we could offer help but were directed by authorities to just wait in the car. So we waited and prayed for all those involved. More than two hours went by, but the time seemed completely unimportant as others struggled for their lives. The sobering thought crossed my mind that had I not run back in for the snow brush, the timing of the car crash may have placed us on the ambulance gurney. We continued to pray for all the workers helping those in need of God's care and all those giving aid.

Once the all clear was given, we inched along the icy, snowy, slick freeway. At one point we needed to use the restroom, so we entered the snow-covered parking lot of a truck stop. After using the facilities and getting something to eat, we again tried to forge forward but promptly got stuck in a snowbank. Several of us helped one another out of the snowdrifts and back onto the road. At this point it was 4:30 a.m. and we still had the majority of the mileage to cover!

An up-close, personal brush with death does a great deal to put one's priorities in perspective. We had no control on if we would arrive for any sleep, the much-needed shower, the radio interview, or even the 8:00 a.m. TV call time. While we value keeping our word, we prize keeping each other safe even more.

Look around. You have a mate! Or maybe you are reading this with someone you care about so much you are planning a wedding with him or her someday. So many people in this world don't have someone to love, or someone who loves them back. Value your partner today just for being alive—and with you.

Lord, help us value every moment of every day together as a gift. Amen.

Relentless

Tell the righteous it will be well with them, for
they will enjoy the fruit of their deeds.
ISAIAH 3:10

We recently spent a weekend in New England and found the weather, the schedule, and the people all *relentless*. Friday night brought torrential rain—the kind that blurs the lines on the road, turns paths into puddles, and soaks your clothes in an instant. Saturday ushered in showers that required rain gear and heavy-duty umbrellas to move anywhere outside through the pounding rain.

The conference schedule didn't alter at all because of the rain. We had to move boxes from the car to the building in the rain on Friday night. We had to dash from our car after setup as buckets of water poured over us. The organizer of the event said to us before we left, "We never let weather dictate what we are going to do. We'll open the doors earlier tomorrow than we'd planned so people can get out of the weather, but we'll stay on schedule!"

And the people showed up. They were eager to learn and full of questions. Every free moment was spent meeting with people, answering their inquiries, and helping them make decisions about resources that would help them build stronger relationships. It was an amazing time of connection as we got to listen to people's stories and build into one another's lives and stories.

It reminded us that we are all building our love lives in the midst of a relentless storm. And personally, we have confidence we can do it because God and His love are *also* relentless. He persistently causes His love to grow in our hearts and He insistently brings His correction when our hearts wander. When the nation of Israel veered off course, concluding they could make it on their own, God persistently applied His discipline:

See now, the Lord, the LORD Almighty, is about to take from Jerusalem and Judah both supply and support: all supplies of food and all supplies of water, the hero and the warrior, the judge and the prophet, the diviner and the elder...The look on their faces testifies against them (Isaiah 3:1-2,9).

He never wants us to settle for self-sufficiency when we have His resources at our disposal, or a limited human perspective when His all-knowing wisdom is available. At the same time, His love constantly pursues the objects of His affection. "Tell the righteous it will be well with them," says Isaiah, "for they will enjoy the fruit of their deeds" (verse 10). God takes a personal interest in making sure the people who respond to His love receive His favor and the resources they need to fulfill their God-given dreams.

This is good news! Our life, like yours, is filled with daily chores, mundane tasks, and challenges that must be overcome. Life's responsibilities feel so relentless. In addition, every day is scattered with moral choices that impact the state of our hearts. When we consider making unhealthy choices, God's discipline confronts the foolishness that threatens to draw us off course. Just as faithfully, God's love rewards us as we pursue habits that foster our love for one another and focus our efforts. When life is relentless, it is nice to know God's love is also relentless toward us.

Next time you're wondering just how relentless God's love is, go read Psalm 136. You'll find the phrase "His love endures forever" repeated 26 times! Today, choose to reflect God's character. Love relentlessly, obey God's Word relentlessly, and get ready for God to bless you relentlessly! His love endures forever!

Lord, give us the longing today to experience Your persistent love more often than Your relentless discipline. Amen.

Day 31

Spiritually Intimate

*Devote yourselves to prayer, keeping alert in it
with an attitude of thanksgiving.*
COLOSSIANS 4:2 NASB

We travel frequently, and we really appreciate staying in the hotels that have peepholes in the doors so that when someone knocks, you can look out and see who's there. Prayer gives us the same opportunity—the chance to look out and see who's really there. People usually aren't phony when praying because it is a time of vulnerability before God. Couples that pray together get a window—a "peephole"—into each other's hearts. You might feel irritated at your spouse all day or you might not understand why they did or said something, but during prayer you get to see what was really going on in their life, their thoughts, and their heart. Prayer gives us a deeper understanding of our mate, and anything that gives a deeper understanding will deepen intimacy. Deeper intimacy creates a safety net for the nakedness of the soul. If you are in a place where you both feel comfortable when your souls are naked before each other, then the physical nakedness that comes within marriage is the next logical step in the sharing of your lives.

Reading the Bible is intimate. The Bible is God's love letter to *each* of us. If you know your spouse is listening to God, your trust level in him or her will grow. If you notice that your spouse is seeking to follow the commands of God, you will feel more relaxed when you are together. God has a complete love for you and when God has your mate's attention, God will steer your spouse into making more loving choices toward you. As a result, the "nagging rate" naturally diminishes. And less nagging and negative corrective language and more positive, affirming language is the cultivated, fertile ground for marital intimacy.

The influence does not stop with your spouse, however. If you are reading the Bible and praying,

God will have your attention and make you a better lover. His love will flow through you to a grateful spouse.

The Holy Spirit is intimate. When we know Christ personally, the Holy Spirit resides in us and gives us the supernatural power to love. It is a supernatural power so that we can love not just with our power, but with God's ability. And since the Holy Spirit indwells anyone who asks Jesus into their life and He knows the way your spouse was designed to be loved, in Him you have the ability to become a great lover for your mate. You will notice that the Holy Spirit gives very specific instructions. He makes it simple enough that your only choice is to obey or disobey. In our life, it may sound something like this:

"Pam, what you said just now to Bill was unkind. He is a good man and he deserves a gentle response."

"Bill, go home. Pam really needs you right now. No, don't finish up that one last task—leave right now."

By reading the Word and praying, you will develop the ability to listen for God's Holy Spirit whisper, and those whispers will help you become a better person and a better partner. These spiritual disciplines will also draw the two of you closer if you make daily use of them as individuals.

Lord, help us make time for prayer, Bible reading, and listening to Your Spirit. We do these things so we might hear Your voice louder than any other.
Amen.

Day 32

Marriage Strong

*You then, my son, be strong in the grace
that is in Christ Jesus.*
2 TIMOTHY 2:1

Our son Zach is a strength and conditioning performance coach at a division one university. For their engagement photo, Zach and his fiancée, Caleigh, chose a word that represents their goal for their future: *strength*. Their wise choice impressed us. It's a great goal for all of us to live a *strong* life— emotionally, physically, relationally, and spiritually. We know it is God's goal for each of us because Psalm 27:14 states it plainly: "Be strong and take heart and wait for the LORD."

But how can we partner with God to gain a strong life?

- "Be strong and very courageous. Be careful to obey all the law my servant Moses gave you; do not turn from it to the right or to the left, that you may be successful wherever you go" (Joshua 1:7)—*Fully obey God's Word.*

- "I long to see you so that I may impart to you some spiritual gift to make you strong—that is, that you and I may be mutually encouraged by each other's faith" (Romans 1:11-12)—*Use your gifts to encourage others and let others encourage you.*

- "Be on your guard; stand firm in the faith; be courageous; be strong. Do everything in love" (1 Corinthians 16:13-14)—*Be vigilant, stand firm in your core beliefs, and do it in love.*

- "Finally, be strong in the Lord and in his mighty power. Put on the full armor of God, so that you can take your stand against the devil's schemes" (Ephesians 6:10-11)—*Wear God's armor (which is the Word).*

- "You then, my son, be strong in the grace that is in Christ Jesus. And the things you have heard me say" (2 Timothy 2:1-2)—*Obey the Word you have heard.*

- "I write to you, young men, because you are strong, and the word of God lives in you" (1 John 2:14)—*Let God's Word live in you.*

Our son Zach was named Ohio's strongest man because of his weight-lifting ability. In a spiritual sense, this world needs more couples who can carry their own weight, help carry the weight of the world, and carry the weight of those who are broken and too weak to carry their own weight. In *Becoming a Woman of Influence*, I share a prayer I prayed for myself, our marriage, and our family: "Lord, let us be like an aircraft carrier. Help our lives be so strong that others can land, get refueled, and restocked. Then let them take off to the mission You have called them to."

Make it your goal to do some spiritual circuit training every day. Pray, read your Bible, memorize Scripture, praise God for His goodness, and share the Good News with others. Your marriage will be stronger, your children will be stronger, and the influence you leave for those around you in your workplace, church, and community will be stronger too. Pump some iron for Jesus!

Lord, make me strong, make us strong, and make our family strong as we daily spend time reading and listening to Your Word and obeying it moment by moment. Amen.

The Answer Is in Your Cell Phone

In your distress you called and I rescued you.
PSALMS 81:7

It happened again today. A friend, a leader, called to say that his marriage was over. My response was sadness and a little curiosity, so I asked, "You had our cell number. Why didn't you call for help?"

The answers we have received over the years included:

- We thought we could handle it (but at some point you must have realized you couldn't).

- We didn't want anyone to know how bad things were (but now the whole world knows of your divorce—that seems worse as far as PR problems go).

- Only one of us wanted help (but even one spouse can make a difference and bring change to a relationship).

- Your friendship matters so much that we didn't want to bring you into our personal lives and problems (I thought friends were supposed to be involved in each other's personal lives).

- We thought it might cost money. (And a divorce is cheap? Counseling is a small investment, and often free or nearly free help is available in a community.)

If you hit a rough patch, pull out your cell phone. Chances are you have at least *one* person in your world that has a strong marriage and would be willing to mentor you. Maybe there's a pastor who would be willing to shepherd you, a therapist willing to counsel you, or a family member willing to walk alongside you.

Shame wants you to sweep issues under the rug. Shame isolates you from those who love and care. Shame helps you make up excuses. But shame is not the voice to listen to. Desperation is a better voice. Be desperate to find the best, most quality, most experienced, or most caring help you can. Be desperate, just like this woman with an "issue" who came to Jesus:

> And a woman was there who had been subject to bleeding for twelve years, but no one could heal her. She came up behind him and touched the edge of his cloak, and immediately her bleeding stopped (Luke 8:43-44).

What were Christ's words to her? Were they words of condemnation? Anger? Frustration? No, He simply said, "Daughter, your faith has healed you. Go in peace" (Luke 8:48). Show that kind of faith. If your marriage hits a rocky patch, pick up your cell phone and call someone. If you can't locate someone willing to help, then call us. We will help you find a clergy member or counselor in your area willing to answer your call for help.

Lord, give us the courage to desperately defend our marriage. Help us combat pride and call out when we need help, knowing You will send someone who cares. Amen.

Day 34

The Garden

"Let us make mankind in our image, in our likeness"…So God created mankind in his own image, in the image of God he created him; male and female he created them.
<small>GENESIS 1:26-27</small>

It was God's plan to make us different from one another from the moment He imagined us. God designed estrogen and testosterone knowing perfectly well just how they would play out in a relationship. Those differences were by design and for a good reason—to complement each other. But sometimes those differences are a quandary to our mate.

When we moved to San Diego, we had a desire to be a light of love to our community. Because both of us were athletes, volunteering in youth sports was a natural place to begin. Bill served as the president of the youth basketball league for eight years. One day at the gym one of the dads walked up to him and said, "I think something is wrong with my wife. I think she might be broken. Can we come in and see you?"

When they arrived, the husband turned to his wife and said, "Go ahead," which seemed to be a green light to begin talking. She began jumping from topic to topic to topic. The husband looked at Bill with a panicked gaze as he said, "She does this all the time."

Bill, knowing social scientists explain the way women interact with life as "integration" (meaning everything connects to everything else), said, "Just think of her mind as a plate of spaghetti. If you look at a plate of spaghetti and follow one noodle around that plate, it looks like it touches every other noodle. She is traveling through her life connecting it to you. Because of this, women are natural multitaskers." Bill taught the husband some listening skills, and his wife talked for 55 straight minutes. Then she sat back and sighed. With a smile she said, "That was great! If I am like spaghetti, then what is he like?"

"Oh, that will be next week," Bill replied, because he wasn't quite sure how he was going to explain how men compartmentalize in a way her husband could easily grasp. Bill began to pray for a food illustration that would depict compartmentalizing. Later that day, our sons were making toaster waffles. Up popped a waffle and Bill thought, "Compartments!"

When the couple returned, Bill explained that men are like waffles because they think of one thing at a time. Each issue goes into its own box or compartment. Because of this, men by nature are problem solvers. They like to go into a box, figure out the problem, apply a solution, and then move on. The husband had an issue that he had tried to solve with his wife for years, and that day Bill was the compartment police. Anytime the wife wanted to hop to a different box, he would bring her back to the original topic. That day they finally solved the issue.

Bill came home and said, "Pam, today I used an illustration in a counseling appointment and it really seemed to help a couple." Then Bill explained to me how men are like waffles and women are like spaghetti. I replied, "Well, it's a little corny, but if it worked, then I trust you, and I trust God. Yes, let's use it at the next conference we teach."

At that conference was a young newlywed couple we had never met before. Afterward the husband introduced himself as the weekend program director of the largest talk radio station in San Diego. The young man asked, "Have you ever thought about radio?" That opportunity turned into a call-in radio program that we hosted for several years, and then a book, *Men Are Like Waffles—Women Are Like Spaghetti,* which has been translated into numerous languages and has consistently been a bestseller in English. We are sure the main reason that so many people seem to connect to the word picture is that it takes couples right back to the Garden. As we go back to the way God designed us, male and female, and we learn to value and appreciate the differences, we can learn to apply those lessons in all of our relationships.

Today, walk yourselves back into the Garden of Eden, back to the way you were both created, and seek to express thanks, appreciation, and value to your mate for the way God created him or her.

Lord, help each of us show visible expressions of appreciation for the way You wired us. Amen.

well-centered children. Aren't those the kind of children you'd like to raise?

We were very proactive in our parenting. We share the details of how we raised our kids in our book *The 10 Best Decisions a Parent Can Make*. The main point is that all along the way we prayed specifically and planned intentionally. We developed a "Learner and Leader Plan," with a yearly Farrel Family Fun Day on which we negotiated privileges and responsibilities. We gave them a gift that applauded their calling each year. We reinforced good choices with a teen relationship contract, an education contract, a driving contract, and a media contract. We added in plenty of fun like father-son trips and individual time with Mom. This way our sons could enjoy their favorite activities while having plenty of time for deeper conversations. At the age of 16 we gave them car keys with this verse on it: "It is God's will that you should be sanctified: that you should avoid sexual immorality; that each of you should learn to control your own body in a way that is holy and honorable" (1 Thessalonians 4:3-4). We also gave each son an ID bracelet with that same verse on it that they wore on dates. Then, as they prepared to launch into their own life, we held a "Walk into Manhood" and invited all their mentors to a celebration. And as they left our home to go to college, we had a "Freshman Foundation Dinner and Dialogue," which was a series of five sets of discussion questions addressing critical issues. (All these are available at our Love-Wise website, www.love-wise.com.)

Sometimes people say, "Bill and Pam, you are so intense." We agree, we are intense—and intentional. Parenting is hard work, but it's a lot easier than *not* doing the work. If you aren't intentional about your parenting, you'll end up having to do a lot more repair work later on because you didn't spend the time sowing right thinking into your children's lives. We just elected to do much of the hard work early so we could enjoy the fruits of having kids who made wise choices as they grew up. As one mentor said to us, "Pay now or pay later—but you will pay."

Bill and I found that working and planning together as parents drew us closer as a couple. And we've only gotten closer as we've watched our sons raising their own families! As a grandmother, I helped author the book *Raising a Modern-Day Princess* because I was motivated to help my granddaughters (and grandsons) make wise choices. As grandparents, we want to back up all the important wisdom our now-grown kids will be passing on to their own children. It's our job to reinforce the values Mom and Dad are sharing.

We know God's desire is for us to be proactive in passing along our values:

> These commandments that I give you today are to be on your hearts. Impress them on your children. Talk about them when you sit at home and when you walk along the road, when you lie down and when you get up. Tie them as symbols on your hands and bind them on your foreheads. Write them on the doorframes of your houses and on your gates (Deuteronomy 6:6-9).

We encourage parents to leave their trademark (™) on their children:

T—Traditions: the things you do yearly to pass on your faith and values.

M—Memories: the special once-in-a-lifetime events or activities that build into your children.

Talk together about what you hope for as your children journey with you. What traditions and memories do you want to give them in order to pass on your belief system?

Lord, help us be proactive in preparing our children well for the life journey You have for them. Give us wisdom and creativity as we plan traditions and memories. Amen.

The Highlight Reel

And Daniel remained there until the
first year of King Cyrus.
DANIEL 1:21

We have been watching our sons compete in athletics for a decade and a half. Over the years we have compiled a number of highlight films to capture the memories of their football exploits. There are great runs, crushing tackles, interceptions run back for touchdowns and game-winning passes. You would think they never lost a game! Watching those films is fun, but they certainly don't capture the whole story. There are no clips of the long hours in the weight room or the long miles of running when no one was watching. There is no footage of time in the training room recovering from injuries. The days of introspection, asking themselves if they should push on and continue to challenge their bodies and minds with the grueling life of an athlete, are missing from the end product. The proof that they did all that is announced in the short but sweet highlights.

Daniel 1:21 is one of those short clips from the life of Daniel that speaks volumes: "And Daniel remained there until the first year of King Cyrus." *There* is in the service of King Nebuchadnezzar advising the ruler of Babylon. What is striking about the statement is that it puts Daniel well into his seventies. The "first year of King Cyrus" was the year the Israelites were given the freedom to rebuild the temple in Jerusalem (Ezra 1:1) and marked the beginning of the end of their 70-year captivity. Daniel was roughly fifteen when he was taken captive, so by verse 21 Daniel has held firm to his convictions and grown in his influence for more than 60 years.

We know he persevered through some very difficult challenges because "Daniel remained." We know he was given wisdom to deliver outstanding advice because "Daniel remained." We know he chose not to compromise over and over again because "Daniel remained." We know he flourished in an environment of jealous opposition because "Daniel remained."

In fact, some of his greatest exploits occurred late in his life. He didn't spend the night with the lions until he was well into his eighties. Daniel 6 begins with the words, "It pleased Darius to appoint 120 satraps to rule throughout the kingdom, with three administrators over them, one of whom was Daniel" (verses 1-2). Darius took over about 19 years after Cyrus, which makes Daniel an old man. He still has great influence and is still strong enough to be perceived as a threat to the other advisors.

The point here is not about age. It is about the value of a lifetime of faithfulness. As a couple, you will have some great years and you will experience some agonizing situations. You will share great victories and you will struggle through strenuous decisions and disappointments. The value of all these shared experiences will be expressed in the fact that *you remained*.

My (Pam's) grandparents were married over 60 years. Some years were very happy; some were pretty stressful. As a couple they endured two world wars, the Great Depression, illnesses, and even some years of poverty, but they hung in together. They remained even when each could have said, "I am not happy." And because they remained, happiness was groomed in their love. I grew up watching my grandfather whisk his bride around the kitchen every Saturday evening as they headed out the door for the evening square dance. Their smiles were broad and their eyes glistened with joy. Remaining produced joy, day after day and year after year, and future generations are still benefiting from their example.

As you look back on your journey, you will not recount every detail or relive every memory. You will, however, remember the highlights that prove you banded together, united your talents, and built a life together.

How is God asking you to remain today? Follow Daniel's example of faithfulness and you will see God be as faithful to you as He was to Daniel in the lions' den.

The Right People

The light of the righteous shines brightly.
PROVERBS 13:9

On our most recent anniversary, I (Bill) wrote this reflective blog:

Today is our anniversary (number 32) and we have been thinking about what has really worked to keep us in love over the years. When I was young, I believed a successful marriage was about finding the right person—the person who would fill in the gaps of your life with an almost magical ability to make you feel stronger. As we have matured, we both now realize it is more about being the right person—the person who can love another human being through the ups and downs of life. In our opinion, "being the right person" means:

- Enjoy the journey. In our relationships we have the potential to create new memories on a regular basis. We are surrounded by responsibilities, difficult decisions, and challenges, and it's easy to lose sight of the fact that every week contains the ability to bring joy to life. Jesus even prayed that this would be true of our lives in John 17:13—"I am coming to you now, but I say these things while I am still in the world, so that they may have the full measure of my joy within them."

- Give grace. We are all imperfect and we live with imperfect people. We have all learned to give ourselves grace in the areas of life that need work. It is much harder for us to be patient and kind with the areas in our spouse's life that need work. If we are going to be successful for the long haul, we will need to be good at forgiving the grievances we hold against each other (Colossians 3:13) and acting "completely humble and gentle" (Ephesians 4:2).

- Laugh often. Marriage is a perfectly imperfect journey with lots of accomplishments, crazy experiences, and funny moments. "A cheerful heart is good medicine, but a crushed spirit dries up the bones" (Proverbs 17:22). Since we can't get it all right, we might as well learn to laugh about it. The moments we laugh about today are the ones we least enjoyed going through at the time. We chuckle about the year-long argument we had. We snicker over the days we didn't know what to do with our kids. We fondly remember the year we didn't have a car and had to ride bikes everywhere we went. These times certainly weren't pleasant when we were living through them, but we now fondly remember them as experiences we would not have had with anyone else on earth.

- Remember your purpose. "For we are God's handiwork, created in Christ Jesus to do good works, which God prepared in advance for us to do" (Ephesians 2:10). Our lives are not accidents and our families are not experiments. God has faithfully been working on our behalf for generations. We are part of a worldwide, history-wide plan being orchestrated by the

God of all creation. As a result, our influence goes at least three generations deep. People we have not even met—and never will meet—will be impacted by the decisions we make today.

We have had more fun being married to each other than we would ever have had on our own. We have also become stronger people because we are married to each other. At one of our banquets with supporters of our nonprofit ministry, we explained the bigger-picture reason for being the right person:

To build a better world, build better nations;

To build better nations, build better cities;

To build better cities; build better churches;

To build better churches, build better families;

To build better families; build better marriages;

To build better marriages, build better partners;

To be a better partner, be a better person!

Jesus, help us be the "right people" so we can be better together, and build a better marriage, family, community, nation, and world. Amen.

When You Love What Must Be Done

In fact, this is love for God: to keep his commands. And his commands are not burdensome.

1 JOHN 5:3

When I (Bill) read today's verse as a young man, it sounded pretty strange. But now that we have a family, it makes a lot more sense. Over the holidays we were privileged to spend time with our kids and grandkids. Since we all live in different cities, there was a lot of work to do to get everyone in the same place. Since our three sons are athletic, there was a lot of work to do to keep everyone fed. And since our grandchildren are four and two years old, there was a lot of work to do just to keep them entertained and to clean up after them! Some of the tasks that were required to make our time together possible were:

- Make airline arrangements

- Prepare the car for travel

- Clean up toys

- Pack the car with five people's suitcases and Christmas presents

- Pack clothes, etc. for a week away from home

- Buy groceries for nine people

- Clean up toys

- Prepare eight dinners, eight lunches, and nine breakfasts for nine people

- Clean up toys

- Do dishes 25 times

- Clean up toys

- Prepare bread to feed ducks, help our grand-daughters get their winter coats on, and walk to the lake

- Carry one of the granddaughters for half a mile

- Clean up toys

- Feed ducks at the lake

- Build a snowman

- Clean up toys

- Help our granddaughters slide down a small snow hill

- Walk back from the lake

- Carry one of the granddaughters uphill for half a mile

- Buy forgotten items

- And did we mention cleaning up toys?

And on it goes…

The amazing thing is that none of this seemed hard because we love the people involved. And that made all the difference. When we are connected to our loved ones and have a mutual environment of love, the work is not burdensome. We simply do what needs to be done without feeling put upon. The Bible calls this *mutual affection,* and it is synonymous with communion or fellowship.[16]

In the same way, when our love for God is clear anything He asks of us seems like a privilege rather than a command. The problem comes when we lose focus or connection. Then we feel used, taken advantage of, and manipulated. The work hasn't changed but the weight of the work certainly feels heavier.

When we love what we do, it doesn't seem like work. We saw this in action over one of the lunches we shared with the family. Two of our sons grabbed a pad of paper and started sketching as they were strategizing about football. One of them is coaching in high school and the other one is playing in college. The coach wanted to sharpen his skill so he was asking the player to help him evaluate their defensive scheme. Technically they were working, but watching them you never would have guessed it. They were animated, energetic, and fully engrossed in the conversation. They love what they do so it was not a burden.

The challenge for us now is to allow discomfort to be a reminder. When the family feels like a burden, it means we have lost connection with them.

When our relationship seems difficult, it means our hearts have drifted. When work feels heavy, it means we have lost sight of the privilege of productivity. When spiritual growth feels like a burden, it means we have lost touch with the love God has for us. The solution is not to run away or further disconnect, but to reengage and reconnect to the deeper relationship. In doing so, our load will be lightened.

Dear Jesus, may our love and Your love overshadow everything we need to do this week! Amen.

You Need Each Other

Do you not know that in a race all the runners run, but only one gets the prize? Run in such a way as to get the prize.
1 CORINTHIANS 9:24

The nation watched intently as Phil and Amy Parham, contestants on NBC's *The Biggest Loser*, lost a combined total of 256 pounds. They went on to author the *90-Day Fitness Challenge*, showing people all across America how to enjoy the benefits of a healthy, active lifestyle. The United States government estimates that a majority of the population is overweight or obese, so the Parhams are really doing their part to help children and grandchildren have their parents and grandparents around for a whole lot longer!

Lest you think we are thin by nature, we too are under doctor's orders to eat a low-sugar, low-carbohydrate, and high-protein diet rich in vegetables and a rainbow of fruits. We both try to gain encouragement from the First Place 4 Health Living Plan. We were both athletes growing up, but as we raised our own sons (all three of them athletes as well) we noticed that we were spending far too much time sitting in the bleachers cheering them on instead of getting up and getting active ourselves. It took a wake-up call in our forties to motivate us to be more faithful to our daily workout. We have now committed to a lifestyle of active dates. We enjoy things like working out at the gym, swimming, tennis, kayaking, and biking together.

Yes, it takes a little work, but it's worth it! Check out God's motivational pep talk:

Do you not know that in a race all the runners run, but only one gets the prize? Run in such a way as to get the prize. Everyone who competes in the games goes into strict training. They do it to get a crown that will not last, but we do it to get a crown that will last forever. Therefore I do not run like someone running aimlessly; I do not fight like a boxer beating the air. No, I strike a blow to my body and make it my slave so that after I have preached to others, I myself will not be disqualified for the prize (1 Corinthians 9:24-27).

Taking great care of each other's health is like training for the Olympics. This passage gives some keys to help you two team up together for greater health and wellness:

Discipline your mind. Keep the goal on the forefront. Run to win the prize; do it for the crown. It is easier to make wise choices if you can remember why you want to make good decisions. Vicki Heath talks about the need for a sustaining motivation in her book *Don't Quit Get Fit: Overcoming the 4 Fitness Killers*. For example, squeezing into your skinny jeans or looking svelte to impress your old football buddies are examples of temporary stimuli. But wanting to live long enough to attend your children's or grandchildren's weddings is the kind of incentive that will last you more than a few weeks.[17] Together, discuss what your sustaining motivation is. What goal do you share that will help you each make wiser choices for your health?

Discipline your body. If you want more years together, you will need to "buffet" your body. You will need strict training. You will need to wear down your body until you have mastery over it. You need to make your body a subjugated servant so that it serves *you,* rather than the other way around. Who wants to be a slave to his or her own body?

We live by an Olympic training center, and we see a great many athletes giving their entire lives over to their sport. These people are focused! If you were an Olympic athlete, you would dedicate great portions of your time to training. As an Olympian, you'd likely get a personal trainer and a workout buddy. You'd need some fans or cheerleaders to keep you motivated. You would make wise choices about food and drink, putting only healthy substances into your body. You would learn to maximize each muscle and strengthen your mind to win the competition.

Be each other's trainer, or at least each other's cheerleader. Talk about how you can help each other make wise choices about your health so you can have a longer happily ever after.

Lord, help us be honest with each other so that together we can live longer and stronger. Amen.

Take T.I.M.E. for Love

*For there is a proper time and procedure for
every matter.*
ECCLESIASTES 8:6

When surveyed, people will always say they don't have enough time. There aren't enough hours in the day! But we are all given the same amount of time: 365 days a year, 7 days a week, and 24 hours a day. Each week contains 168 hours. If you follow medical advice and get the recommended 8 hours of sleep a night, you've used up 56 hours. That leaves you with 112 hours to fit in work, exercise, meals, socializing, family time, and romance.

Here is God's slant on time:

Be very careful, then, how you live—not as unwise but as wise, making the most of every opportunity, because the days are evil (Ephesians 5:15-16).

We live in evil days, so God wants us to prioritize our time well. Let's make things clear. It was God who created marriage, way back in Genesis with Adam and Eve. So marriage was a priority relationship from the very beginning. Marriage was created before church, before community, before business. Marriage is on the heart of God, so you have permission to prioritize time for yours! Schedule in T.I.M.E. for love.

How much time does it take to stay in love for a lifetime? In our book *Red-Hot Monogamy,* we explain the minimum time commitment necessary to maintain the connectedness and a strong, healthy marriage (and a sizzling sex life). Make some T.I.M.E. for love:

Ten to twenty minutes to talk together *alone* every day. It is amazing how just making time to talk together (about things more important than who is going to pick up the milk) will reconnect and rekindle your hearts. This is the reason that we place couple communication questions in all of the books we author.

Many of the most happily married couples we know—those with a sparkle in their eyes after 30, 40, and even 50 years together—have found the magic in the small things: a cup of coffee and conversation in the morning or a walk around the block in the evening.

Invest in a weekly date night (or date breakfast or lunch) together for at least 4 hours. (It takes a couple hours to emotionally reconnect.) We believe in the weekly date time so much that we actually schedule two of these a week. Sometimes life interrupts the best-laid plans, so having twice as much time as we actually feel we need for each week's date ensures that even on the busiest weeks we get at least the minimum.

Make a monthly day-away policy. At least once a month spend eight to twelve uninterrupted hours together. This is an important commitment, and you can spend the time doing anything you *both* enjoy. Sometimes parents of young children find it difficult to find overnight childcare, but it doesn't cost anything to get creative! Once you've put the kids to bed, you can turn your own home into a B&B and make it seem like you "got away." And by finding a new sport or hobby you both enjoy, you create some common bonds.

Escape quarterly (or at least biannually). Get away from home for a 24- to 48-hour weekend. If possible, spend one of the getaways taking in a conference where you can learn new tools to strengthen your marriage. Spend the other getaways just resting, relaxing, and rejuvenating together. This can be worked into a family vacation, but be sure you get at least 24 hours of alone time if you mix this retreat in with spending time with family. Nothing is as nice as unplugging from life and cuddling up *alone* to stir the embers of love.

Above all, remember to enjoy your T.I.M.E.!

Lord, give us the wisdom to make time for us.
Amen.

Day 41

Decisive Influence

Fathers, do not exasperate your children;
instead, bring them up in the training and
instruction of the Lord.
EPHESIANS 6:4

Today's verse has at its heart the tremendous influence couples have as parents. "Child training" is built around the idea of disciplining children until they develop *self*-discipline. The goal is to raise up self-directed adults who possess self-control. Early on, children lack this ability. It's our responsibility as parents to make decisions for them…and then gradually release the responsibility to them as they demonstrate that they are ready.

Instruction literally means "training by word." This coaching and training can include the use of whatever means are necessary to get results. It can, therefore, include teaching, reproof, challenges, reminders, and growth strategies. The goal is to help the sons and daughters we love discover their God-given dreams and develop the skills necessary to live them out. As parents, we are trying to help our kids develop self-discipline and to live out their potential. If we want to maximize our impact on our kids and grandkids then, we need to give them as much decision-making authority as they can handle.

This was especially clear to us as our middle son, Zach, was getting ready to enter high school. Like many younger siblings, Zach wanted to create an identity separate from his older brother's. However, he took this desire a little too far! His motto in life became, "If Brock likes it, then I'm going to hate it!" I (Bill) asked him, "What do you want to do when you get to high school?"

"I don't know, but I don't want to be like Brock," he said.

"Do you want to play football?"

"No."

"Why not?"

"Because Brock plays football."

"Do you want to be in student leadership?"

"No."

"Why not?"

"Because Brock is in student leadership."

This went on forever and despite our best efforts, we couldn't get him to decide which extracurricular activities he wanted to pursue. We knew that if he entered the turbulent high school years with this attitude, it would not go well. In desperation, we had a sit-down meeting with him.

"Zachery, the way you are thinking about your life right now is not good. You keep telling us who you *don't* want to be, but you aren't deciding who you *do* want to be. We can't really trust you right now to make the right decisions, so we need to take action. You have a choice. You can either change the way you are approaching this or Dad can go to high school with you."

We knew the message got across because his eyes got as big as basketballs. You could hear the thoughts racing through his mind: "You wouldn't do that, would you? That would be so embarrassing. I would be the biggest loser in my school."

We were desperately praying he would change because the last thing I (Bill) wanted to do was go back to high school! It didn't take Zach long to make a decision. He did play football in high school, and then he did something his oldest brother would never consider. He became a competitive cheerleader, and his success in this sport eventually led to a college scholarship. It is not what I would have chosen but it was a great path for him. He just needed a little coaching to get to his success.

If you have children, discuss with your spouse how you can team up to better coach your kids toward their unique, God-ordained path.

Lord, give us both wisdom to make decisions that develop self-control. Help us and our children reach our full potential. Amen.

Treasure the Unexpected

*Blessed is he who comes in
the name of the Lord!*
MATTHEW 21:9

Some of the best memories in life happen when you least expect them. We recently spoke at a large conference in Edmonton, Canada, where we saw more than our share of transformation in a short period of time. Three couples said to us, "We were separated when we came here. If this didn't work, we weren't too sure what we were going to do. But we've had a breakthrough at the conference this week and we have found our motivation again."

Another couple told us, "We realized this week-end that we haven't been doing what will really help us. We are a blended family and we have resorted to blaming each other for our problems. We are going to start by reading one of your books together and practicing the new skills you've been teaching here."

Those were the comments we kind of expected to hear. We had prayed for this kind of movement in people's lives and amazingly, that kind of transformation happens regularly at marriage conferences. What we didn't expect was the inspiration that came from the ride to the airport at the end of the conference.

The man who drove the SUV appeared to be an ordinary volunteer. There was nothing striking about his appearance and he was humbly serving as a driver for the conference. As we headed out, we discovered that Paul was a member of a singing quartet called the Crew Guys. He has a natural ear for music and is something of an expert at speaking in dialects. In the short ride, he sang a pitch-perfect a capella version of "Turn Your Eyes upon Jesus" and then entertained us by speaking in dialects from Ireland, Newfoundland, England, and a Southern California beach community. We laughed, applauded, and marveled that such a gifted man was content to be a humble servant for the weekend. After a long weekend of giving of ourselves for ministry, he gave of himself to entertain us! This was an unexpected treasure, an unanticipated blessing from God to our hearts.

Matthew 21 begins with the story of one of the greatest unexpected treasures in history. It was the beginning of the Passover week and people were flocking to Jerusalem to celebrate the holiday. They had done this year after year, and everyone knew the routine. They made their plans and set their expectations for the week. But Jesus was about to do something no one could have anticipated. He "sent two disciples, saying to them, 'Go to the village ahead of you, and at once you will find a donkey tied there, with her colt by her. Untie them and bring them to me'" (verses 1-2). The disciples did as He'd asked, bringing the donkey and the colt and placing their cloaks on them for Jesus to sit on.

And then something even more unexpected happened. A very large crowd spread their cloaks on the road along the path that Jesus was going to take, while others cut branches from the trees and spread them out in front of Him. The crowds that went ahead of Him and those that followed shouted:

"Hosanna to the Son of David!"

"Blessed is he who comes in the name of the Lord!"

"Hosanna in the highest heaven!"

As Matthew tells it, "When Jesus entered Jerusalem, the whole city was stirred and asked, 'Who is this?' The crowds answered, 'This is Jesus, the prophet from Nazareth in Galilee'" (verses 10-11).

The highlight of their day was the unexpected entrance of the Messiah.

What can we learn from this story? First, be faithful in the daily things and the activities that seem mundane. Second, keep your eyes open to the unexpected blessings and kisses from heaven that God will send your way. Soon you and your mate will share an unexpected moment together that may become one of the highlights of your year. When it happens, remember to shout, "Hosanna!"

Walk Away Together

For the upright will live in the land, and the blameless will remain in it; but the wicked will be cut off from the land, and the unfaithful will be torn from it.

PROVERBS 2:21-22

While we were writing this devotional, Whitney Houston, often called the Queen of Pop, was found dead in her hotel room the night before the Grammy Awards. Whitney, who started singing as a small girl in a gospel choir at church, rose to superstardom and then married Bobby Brown (who was infamous at the time for his bad-boy personality). Soon the pair became known for their hard drug-using party lifestyle and tumultuous—and sometimes violent—relationship. In the end, they lost their marriage, Whitney lost her stellar voice, and ultimately lost her life.

You might be thinking, "Oh, that would never happen to us." But ask yourself if there are any areas where you are causing your mate to stumble, or places where you are leading your mate off God's best path for your marriage. Perhaps you have said something like:

- Let's have a little wine. We work hard; we deserve it. (Then one glass turns into a full-blown alcohol addiction, and eventually one of you finds yourself in rehab.)

- Come on, let's order pizza and polish off a gallon of ice cream. (This can create a pattern of poor eating habits that will end up destroying your good health.)

- We're in a rut in the bedroom. Let's watch some porn, it will spice thing up. (Porn then becomes addictive and you can't get aroused without it.)

- We need to relax. Let's party. It's just a little marijuana. Don't be so uptight, try it. (Eventually you'll find yourself prey to an escalating and almost unstoppable pattern of drug abuse.)

- They are going to pay us under the table so we don't have to pay taxes. (Eventually it will become easier and easier to cut corners in business and finances.)

- Come on, let's just take a few things off the store rack and not pay for them. It's a big corporation—they won't miss it and we need it. (Then a pattern of shoplifting and stealing develops and you find yourself in jail.)

Watch out for a couple of key phrases in your rationalizations: *We deserve it* and *we need it.* Yes, you might deserve healthy things like a day off, a good night's sleep, or couple time away from the heavy responsibilities you carry. However, it is deceptively easy to think you need or deserve things that are *not* healthy. Seriously, do you really *need* wine, drugs, porn, or a consistent diet of sugar and fast food? No. You *need* things like good health, close communion with family and friends, and a close relationship with each other and God.

The Bible gives great advice when it warns:

You were running well; who hindered you from obeying the truth? This persuasion did not come from Him who calls you. A little leaven leavens the whole lump of dough (Galatians 5:7-9 NASB).

If you don't think your small compromises will catch up to you, consider an article I (Pam) keep on my desk about a couple who were once colleagues and good friends. We all went to seminary at the same time, did youth work at the same time, and headed into the senior pastorate at the same time. Bill and I took very careful steps to protect our relationship, guard our personal integrity, and fortify our ministry with selective choices to shield our reputation. Our mantra was "be above reproach." Our colleagues, on the other hand, began to indulge in a "we work hard so God wants us to reward ourselves" lifestyle. It began with seemingly harmless toys like jet skis, vacation homes, and a new Jacuzzi—all very innocent and benign choices. But the attitude of "we deserve it" soon slid into "we are above the rules."

Pride entered in and they began to drink excessively and watch porn. This lifestyle escalated into sex with other partners. It all came crashing down when photos of their now perverted choices leaked into the public sphere through social media. They lost their ministry, their marriage, their health, the respect of their children, and their place of esteem in the community. Not quite the happily ever after we all hope for, is it?

Watch out for that little bit of leaven. Indulging small sins is like adding a teaspoon of arsenic to your dinner: Eventually it will catch up to you and kill the bright future you dream of.

Lord, help me influence my mate to choose well and right. Guard our hearts against the small sins that can escalate into big trouble. Amen.

Yes! Tonight I Have a Headache

Stop depriving one another, except by agreement for a time, so that you may devote yourselves to prayer, and come together again so that Satan will not tempt you because of your lack of self-control.

1 Corinthians 7:5 NASB

I (Pam) remember praying about this command in First Corinthians one day. My prayer went something like, *Lord, You know I absolutely love sex with Bill. He is so awesome. But God, You also know I struggle with migraines. I want to say yes to Bill as much as possible but God, I get these headaches and that is such a cliché excuse. "Not tonight, I have a headache." Can You solve this for me, God?*

Shortly after that prayer, I had a doctor's appointment for my migraines. As I sat in the waiting room, I read a medical magazine with a small article in it that said sex opens up the blood vessels, and it actually lessens the pain of migraines! So now I have changed my response. Now it is, "Yes, honey! Tonight I have a headache." It is much more fun to reach for Bill when I feel a headache coming on than to reach for a bottle of pain reliever!

Sex and prayer are the two best tools to keep Satan from tempting you as a couple. One church had us come in to speak on red-hot monogamy because a female leader with a negative attitude toward her spouse and intimacy was teaching that if you wanted to be truly "spiritual" as a wife you would abstain from sex with your husband—for years! When the leadership caught wind of this unbiblical teaching they asked us to come share a more balanced biblical view.

According to today's verse, yes, there might be times when you need to "devote yourselves to prayer" and abstain from sex. Perhaps you need to spend time fasting and praying as a couple instead as you seek wisdom on a job opportunity, a move, or how to handle a health issue or a wayward, hard-to-raise child. But this would be a brief time of intense spiritual focus that should then be followed up with some intense one-on-one time behind the bedroom door.

One of the most spiritual acts of obedience that you as a husband or wife can perform is to give yourself with a full heart and a willing body. Lavish love on your spouse! Sex was created *for* marriage, and it should be treated as seriously in your schedule as any of the other spiritual disciples like a devotional quiet time, going to church on the weekend, or prayer. God is pretty serious when He says, "stop depriving one another." This phrase can also be translated as, "stop defrauding." When you made your wedding vows, you were saying "I do" to a lifetime of partnership—and that included sex! If you are physically able but mentally unwilling to become a willing participant, then it is the same as telling God you don't think prayer is important either. Red-hot monogamy is a priority in marriage.

Look at the context of today's verse. The verses preceding the command not to deprive each other of intimacy is packed with instruction on this topic:

The husband must fulfill his duty to his wife, and likewise also the wife to her husband. The wife does not have authority over her own body, but the husband does; and likewise also the husband does not have authority over his own body, but the wife does (1 Corinthians 7:3-4 NASB).

In a Christian marriage, we are called to "fulfill our duty" to each other. In this verse, the word "duty" could also be translated as the "debt" or the "should-do" of marriage. As for the part about "you must fulfill," in this context the verb can also mean "to pay, to give a reward," or "to bear fruit." Those are all good things, right? We all love a paycheck and would happily accept a reward, and we are grateful to eat luscious yummy fruit—so emotionally, God is saying that sex should be viewed as a duty you want to fulfill! And the best part? The verb tense of "fulfill" makes it clear that we should make a habit of it!

Verse 4 is really the key to success at a fulfilling sex life. A husband and wife have mutual authority over each other's bodies! When we stood up and made our wedding vows, we committed to give 100 percent of ourselves to love our mate, and we *both* made this commitment. When we understand this, it becomes natural to desire to give of ourselves in the bedroom too.

Lord, give us drive and the desire to be with each other intimately. Amen.

You Are Not Going to Like It

Above all, love each other deeply, because love covers over a multitude of sins.
1 PETER 4:8

I (Pam) am an enthusiastic entrepreneur at heart. I have a desire to create something from nothing, providing quality resources and products that bless and build other people's lives while providing for my own family. When Bill was new in his senior pastor position at the age of 28, I was a mom at home while completing my education at the same time. I knew my school bills were a stress on our already shoestring budget, so I attended a motivational seminar for those interested in running their own businesses. The presenter was very persuasive and I bought the magic beans.

However, on the way home, I was convicted by the Holy Spirit because I had spent more than our agreed-upon amount. As newlyweds, Bill and I set a dollar amount we could each spend without checking in with the other. For any purchase over that amount, we were supposed to call each other and ask for approval. We would decide together if this was how *we* wanted to spend *our* money. I had violated that trust. I prayed and asked God to forgive me, and then I asked for wisdom about the best way to break the news to Bill in hopes that he would also forgive me.

I walked in and took Bill's hand. I looked him in the eyes and with emotion I said, "I have something to tell you, and you are not going to like it. But please tell me, 'I love you and we will get through this together.'" All kinds of thoughts of worst-case scenarios swirled around in his mind. As I told him the story he felt relieved, but then I could see the anger rising. To his credit, through gritted teeth he said, "Pam, I love you, I forgive you, and we will get through this together." The mercy Bill showed lodged deep in my heart and a deeper love for my husband grew.

Years later, my father passed away and left me an inheritance. Bill had a person he trusted offer him "an incredible investment opportunity." So Bill committed my inheritance and talked me into the investment as a great safeguard to our future. In our culture today people are a bit skeptical of investment advisors because of the infamous Bernie Madoff, who orchestrated the largest financial fraud scam in U.S. history, defrauding customers of over 20 billion dollars. However, we experienced this long before all the "buyer beware" warnings had gone out. And unfortunately, we had our own Madoff-like experience when Bill learned the investment was completely gone. He was disheartened at the financial failure, and he felt especially bad because the lost money had been the inheritance my father left me. He prayed about the best way to break the news to me.

He walked in, took my hands in his, and with emotion in his eyes he said, "Pam, I have something to tell you, and you are not going to like it. But I need you to tell me, 'I love you and we will get through this together.'" Now my error was in the hundreds of dollars, and Bill's was in the thousands of dollars. But remembering Bill's grace and mercy from years before my heart pushed out the words, "Bill, I love you, I forgive you, and we will get through this together."

On both occasions, because of our honesty and forgiveness of each other our teamwork became stronger. Economically we have more than recovered. Grace, mercy, and forgiveness create an environment where love can accumulate interest just like money in an investment account. In that environment both of you can flourish emotionally, spiritually, and perhaps even financially because you will be teaming up together on your journey.

Lord, help us give grace and mercy to cover each other's imperfections. Amen.

Day 46

You Gotta Have Friends

The righteous choose their friends carefully.
PROVERBS 12:26

I (Pam) recently upgraded to a new computer. I was trying to type a letter and must have accidentally hit a wrong button because all the codes that tell a computer what to do were appearing in the text. Knowing I couldn't send a letter that looked like that, I grabbed my laptop and headed for Bill's office. (He's usually able to fix my technical problems!) He was in the middle of a relationship coaching session with a couple named Steve and Beth, but he could read the distress on my face as I walked up. He graciously invited me in and introduced me to the couple. I then, very emotionally, pleaded my case and begged for some help with my dilemma. I was a little relieved that Bill couldn't figure out what I had done or how to undo it either! Although he couldn't fix the problem, his confusion made me feel like I wasn't as dumb as I looked!

Then an amazing thing happened. Beth said, "Would you like me to try? I'm a computer programmer." Within about one second, after one mouse click, she fixed the issue and told me how to fix it in the future. Then she said, "I have the training that helps me understand computer codes. You both have the training to help us understand relationship codes. Knowing the code makes all the difference."

In our book *The Marriage Code*, we explain how to unlock love. The interaction with Beth explains one key component: friendship and love. It is wise to get people around you who know what they are doing in the area of love, romance, and commitment. One study we read said that couples who share a long-lasting love tend to surround themselves with friends who also believe in long-lasting love. In our experience, the mutual support that comes from friendships like these can be a huge factor in the success of a marriage!

As newlyweds our best friends were a couple named Steve and Grace. We worked in ministry together, socialized together, and supported each other's marriages by attending church, seminars, and other marriage-building activities. Bill and I have also cultivated our friendships with our siblings and their spouses so that at family gatherings, our conversations will often turn to love, romance, and marriage. We attend (or usually lead) Sunday school classes and small groups that study marriage topics. When we moved to a new area and couldn't find a group that focused on marriage and family, we'd start a small group for this purpose.

Friends can help unlock love in at least three ways:

See no evil. Observing how couples serve each other in love (the opposite of being selfish) can help you decide how to extend kindness and hospitality to your mate.

Hear no evil. Listening to the words of encouragement (or words that cut) will help you decide what your vocabulary will be.

Speak no evil. Watching others communicate by strategically using a specific tone of voice or body language can help you enhance your own communication. Even if you see your friends making mistakes, you can make mental notes to not repeat that pattern.

When you hit tough times or a rough patch in your marriage, don't flee to single friends who have their own baggage or a chip on their shoulders toward marriage. Instead seek out married friends who have weathered a few storms and survived. They're the people who know how to help you out of the rut you're in! Look for friends who will be a safety net for your marriage, providing love and wisdom for your future. Glean knowledge from couples whose love has stood the test of time.

Lord, help us be wise in choosing the friends to surround our love, home, and marriage. Amen.

Your Love Is a Light

*A new command I give you: Love one another.
As I have loved you, so you must love one
another. By this everyone will know that you
are my disciples, if you love one another.*

JOHN 13:34-35

People are wondering if anyone really has the real deal. They are asking, "Does knowing God really impact a love relationship or marriage?" Let us assure you—your love is a light! Let us share an example from our life:

Bill was a pastor and we were new to the community with two young children. I was expecting our third son when I met Trina in the bleachers at a baseball game. She was about as far from God as a woman could be. She had three children fathered by three different men. She hadn't been married to any of them. At the time she was pregnant and living with a condom salesman (are you catching the irony of this situation?). She would come to me with all kinds of spiritual questions, like, "Hey, I got this flyer at the grocery store. It says the incarnation of Jesus is going to be at the Coliseum being channeled through some guru. Do you want to go see Jesus?" or "I think I know God's will for my life. I went to see a palm reader—want to know what she said?"

One day, after helping her through yet another of her many questions from her very colorful rainbow of spiritual experiences, I said, "Trina, it seems like you have lots of questions about God and what His role should be in your life. I love answering your questions, but maybe you would enjoy a study that will actually walk you through who God is, who Jesus is, and how He loves you and has a great plan for your life. Want to come to my home for a Bible study once a week? Then after the study time we could take the kids to the park or the beach. Interested?" She was very interested.

She showed up for our study sessions, but after a few months I still couldn't see any big spiritual movement in her life. I was pulling out all the great tools like *A Case for Christ*, *Evidence That Demands a Verdict*, and *The Uniqueness of Jesus*. Yet she was still resistant to make the decision to give her heart to Jesus and let God love her. That is, until one day when she was in our home—watching us. Bill had our only car as the other one was in the shop getting fixed.

Now, we often teach an important principle: "The thing you love about your mate can become a source of irritation. That thing you first fell in love with can end up driving you crazy, so you need a way to remember, *Oh yeah, that is why I love him or her.*" One thing I love about Bill is that he is a great listener. He treats each person he speaks with as if they are the only person in the room. But because of this he never checks his watch, so he usually runs ten or fifteen minutes late—thus my irritation. Because he knows this about himself, he has created a new habit of running by the corner flower stand by our home where you can purchase a dozen short-stem roses for five dollars. He figures, "If I am going to be late anyway, I might as well make a big entrance with flowers—it kind of takes Pam's edge off when I walk in with roses."

So on this afternoon he waltzed in with these flowers, gave me a kiss, and said, "Love you, babe. Can I help you ladies load the van for the beach?"

Trina looked at me and said, "Did your Jesus make him bring you those flowers?" I replied, "Yeah, I guess you could say that. God's Spirit does help each of us do things to stay in love."

Then Trina said, "Okay, now I want to know your Jesus!"

Make a list of people you think are watching the way you are dating or how in love you are in your marriage. Begin to pray that your love will be a light of God's love to these people.

Lord, let us love how You love so that we can light the path to You. Amen.

Battle Weary

*I am giving you this command in keeping with
the prophecies once made about you, so that by
recalling them you may fight the battle well.*
1 TIMOTHY 1:18

Life is a battle. But what you might not realize is
that your love life is the frontline. We can get morally exhausted just trying to keep doing the right
thing. The world says that when your mate offends
you, you have the right to get back at him or her.
You even have the right to leave the marriage! But
God challenges you to remain—to stay and fight for
your marriage. The Bible says, "God is love" (1 John
4:8). And because God is love, Satan hates it when

we are in love. He will try anything to drive a wedge between the two of you. You might really want a love that lasts, but it is easy to get battle-weary and not stay vigilant in the fight to protect our love. It is easy to get weary in doing well.

But don't give up. Jesus has your back in the battle! There is a promise waiting for us as we press forward in love:

> Let us not become weary in doing good, for at the proper time we will reap a harvest if we do not give up. Therefore, as we have opportunity, let us do good to all people, especially to those who belong to the family of believers (Galatians 6:9-10).

> And the God of all grace, who called you to his eternal glory in Christ Jesus, after you have suffered a little while, will himself restore you and make you strong, firm, and steadfast. To him be the power forever and ever. Amen (1 Peter 5:10-11).

In His sovereignty God has committed to rebuild us after the attacks. We are told that He will:

- restore—to mend, to put in order, to make one what he ought to be

- establish—to make stable

- strengthen—to make one strong

- support—to lay the foundation

The result of His actions is that we are restored from previous attacks and prepared for future. We have seen God faithfully repeat this process over and over again in our lives. But let us share the steps of how God proves this to His people in Exodus 16:11-24:

1. God notices the stress of the Israelites (verses 11-12). "The LORD said to Moses, 'I have heard the grumbling of the Israelites. Tell them, "At twilight you will eat meat, and in the morning you will be filled with bread. Then you will know that I am the LORD your God."'"

2. God takes steps to reduce the stress of the Israelites (verses 13-21). "That evening quail came and covered the camp, and in the morning there

was a layer of dew around the camp. When the dew was gone, thin flakes like frost on the ground appeared on the desert floor...Moses said to them, 'It is the bread the LORD has given you to eat'....Each morning everyone gathered as much as they needed, and when the sun grew hot, it melted away."

3. God makes rest a priority in the midst of their stress (verse 23). Through the mouth of Moses, God told the Israelites, "Tomorrow is a day of complete rest, a holy Sabbath to the LORD."

Lord, when we are weary, restore and rebuild us so we can stay in love for a lifetime. Amen.

Fun to the Core

A cheerful heart is good medicine.
PROVERBS 17:22

Bill and I have so much fun together, and everyone can tell! Lifeway interviewed us on how to cultivate humor, fun, and delight in a marriage. When the pressure is on, disappointments are too numerous to count, and frustrations are escalating faster than an elevator in a skyrise, we have chosen to cultivate the art of joy. We trade jokes and e-mail humor, or slide funny cards into each other's luggage or under our office doors. We started on this road of frivolity as newlyweds. We'd hide squirt guns all over the house and spontaneously break into a squirt gun fight. We look for humor from clean comedians and in the daily living of life, like when our four-year-old granddaughter opened her Christmas present—a princess backpack—and exclaimed with glee, "I have waited my whole life for this!"

And even when things go wrong, we look for the humor in the crisis. Like the time Bill forgot his dress suit pants when we traveled to perform a wedding. The picture in our mind of a pastor doing a wedding in his boxer shorts just gave us the giggles. (It made the frantic pursuit to find slacks in only 40 minutes an adventure!)

In my (Pam's) book *LOL with God*, my coauthor, Dawn Wilson, and I chronicle just a few of the over 350 verses that speak to joy:

- 1 Chronicles 16:27—"Strength and joy are in his dwelling place." (Dwell with God and find joy!)

- Job 33:26—"Then that person can pray to God and find favor with him, they will see God's face and shout for joy." (Pray, and joy will be reignited.)

- Psalm 5:11—"Let all who take refuge in you be glad; let them ever sing for joy." (Hide your heart in God, and joy will erupt in song.)

- Psalm 35:27—"May those who delight in my vindication shout for joy and gladness; may they always say, 'The LORD be exalted, who delights in the well-being of his servant.'" (Rejoice in God's righteousness, and justice and joy will return.)

- Psalm 71:23—"My lips will shout for joy when I sing praise to you—I whom you have delivered." (Worship God for His redeeming love, and joy will naturally evolve.)

- Psalm 92:4—"You make me glad by your deeds, LORD; I sing for joy at what your hands have done." (Review the goodness of God, and joy will fill your mind and roll off your lips.)

- Psalm 118:15—"Shouts of joy and victory resound in the tents of the righteous: 'The LORD'S right hand has done mighty things!'" (Review God's victories, and joy will accompany the "rerun" of love.)

- Psalm 145:7—"They will celebrate your abundant goodness and joyfully sing of your righteousness." (Throw a party to celebrate God's provision, and joy will be the centerpiece of your life.)

- Proverbs 21:15—"When justice is done, it brings joy to the righteous." (Do the right thing, and joy will stick.)

- Jeremiah 15:16—"When your words came, I ate them; they were my joy and my heart's delight." (Get into God's Word—joy is there!)

We have discovered that cultivating joy empowers our marriage. We don't spend valuable time paralyzed by depression, entangled in arguments, or frenzied by frustrations. Joy rescues love when circumstances creep in that threaten to zap the energy of your life and love. In those times we have discovered that the "joy of the Lord is [our] strength" (Nehemiah 8:10). When life gets tough, band together and head to Jesus, and you will be able to echo what King David says: "In Your presence is fullness of joy" (Psalms 16:11 NASB).

God, when things get hard help us run to You, the source of all joy. Then, Lord, help us team up to hold on to the joy You give. Amen.

Go Get 'Em, God!

*Our gospel came to you not simply with
words but also with power, with the Holy
Spirit and deep conviction.*
1 Thessalonians 1:5

God's Spirit works in connection with God's
Word and your heart. Jesus explains that "when
he, the Spirit of truth, comes, he will guide you
into all the truth" (John 16:13). Often, a verse you
come across in the Bible will be exactly what you
need to gain the access code to your mate's heart.
This verse will help you to move above what we call
"the line of trust" to the place where love and life are
good. Today's passage might be such a verse! God is

faithful to lead you in all truth in your years as new-lyweds and long into your marriage.

Recently, Bill and I found ourselves out of rhythm with one another. Bill was transitioning from a wonderful position with Dr. David Jeremiah as a small groups pastor and beginning to work with me full-time as an author and speaker. We were both excited at the opportunity to work together to help people become "Love-Wise." However, Bill missed the church setting and the camaraderie of working with the leaders who were on staff at that mega-church. I, on the other hand, was thrilled to hand Bill a very long to-do list of the things that were lined up waiting for his wisdom and expertise.

But Bill wasn't working as quickly on my list as I'd hoped. He was still emotionally processing and acclimating to this new environment and routine. I became frustrated by the many tasks still remaining on Bill's to-do list—things that I thought should have been checked off days ago. In short, I allowed fear to sneak in the back door. I was afraid that Bill would let me down and want to return to the bi-vocational lifestyle, and I would once again have to share Bill's valuable time with another organization.

I (Bill) was frustrated by what seemed to me to be Pam's unrealistic expectations. I was afraid that I would never be able to live up to her demands on me.

There had been an underlying cooling of the temperature of our relationship over a few days, and I (Pam) began to pray that God would show me who needed to change and own the issue. I secretly hoped that Bill would get all convicted so I'd get a heartfelt apology. I could then valiantly forgive him, and I wouldn't have to change anything on the to-do list I'd written for him!

One morning I left for the gym, and on the way there I prayed, "God, go after Bill. Get him in gear! Get his attention!"

I often listen to *Walk the Word* music that I've downloaded onto my iPod because I know the Spirit has an easier time moving us in truth when we are in the Truth. That day at the gym I was listening to the *New Testament Experience*, and there, piped into my headphones, was a wonderfully irritating insight.

Ephesians 4:1-3 was dramatically read into my heart: "As a prisoner for the Lord, then, I urge you to live a life worthy of the calling you have received. Be completely humble and gentle; be patient, bearing with one another in love. Make every effort to keep the unity of the Spirit through the bond of peace."

God's Spirit gently asked me, *Have you been humble toward Bill, or have you already decided this has to be Bill's fault? Have you been gentle? Patient? Have you been bearing with him and the huge pile of responsibilities on his plate coming from all different directions? When was the last time you said* thank you *instead of barking out orders or e-mailing requests for action? Pam, have you made every effort to bless Bill? Every effort to encourage Bill? Every effort to lower his stress? Every effort to meet his emotional needs? You are a relationship specialist, so you know better. Have you really been living a life worthy of your calling? Pam, pause for a moment, right here in this gym, and pray. Ask Me what you can do for Bill that will help him feel My love, My plan, and My hope. The way to your hope, Pam, is to meet Bill's needs right now rather than have him meet yours.*[18]

I was praying God would go after Bill so our marriage would get back on track again, "above the line of trust." Instead, God pinpointed exactly what I needed to do to bless our relationship. I came home, gave Bill a big hug, and said, "I know this has been quite a transition for you and I know that in my excitement, I have been very demanding with my long list. I'm sorry. Please forgive me—and please know I fully trust you to work in your way, in your time." My apology moved us above that "line of trust" because I became easier to live with and easier to love.

Spirit, please lead us moment by moment to truth as we are in the Truth of Your Word. Amen.

I Do!

Servants in the church are to be
committed to their spouses.
1 TIMOTHY 3:12 MSG

As we write this, we are planning a wedding! No, not for us—we have been happily married for over 32 years. This joyous nuptial is between our middle son and his precious fiancée. Our conversations with them cover vital topics like premarital counseling and God's design for marriage, but we are also chatting about invitations, caterers, reception halls, flower bouquets, dress and tux styles, and a myriad of other details for their big celebration. But when it comes right down to it, most of the wedding hoopla

227

is just wrapping paper around what is *truly* vital: the vows.

If you are married, close your eyes and remember how you felt on your own wedding day. If you are headed to the altar, picture yourself standing in front of your family and friends and saying those words. They are so important that the people you love most will interrupt their normal lives to witness you voicing them.

When the two of you said (or will say!) *I do*, you were making this promise:

I promise to take you, to have and to hold from this day forward, to love and to cherish, for better or for worse, for richer, for poorer, in sickness and in health, forsaking all others, I promise to keep only to you, from this day forward, until death do us part.

Let's break down those promises—the commitment and the covenant you made that day:

To have and to hold. This phrase reminds us of Jesus's words in Luke 10:27: "Love the Lord your

God with all your heart and with all your soul and with all your strength and with all your mind; and, Love your neighbor as yourself." The promise also brings to mind Colossians 3:23: "Whatever you do, work at it with all your heart, as working for the Lord, not for human masters." Both these verses share an "all in" attitude, showing us what it means to be fully committed.

From this day forward. Marriage is a daily, moment-by-moment decision to love. One verse that shares this emphasis on "daily" is Hebrews 3:13: "But encourage one another daily, as long as it is called 'Today,' so that none of you may be hardened by sin's deceitfulness." Daily means just that: Love, encourage, build up, and strengthen each other each and every day.

To love and to cherish. Love is a verb. The biblical picture of *agape* means to love your mate unconditionally. Love when it's easy as well as when it's hard. *Cherish* each other and take care of each other the ways Ephesians 5:29 describes: "For no one ever hated his own flesh, but nourishes and cherishes it, just as Christ also does the church" (NASB).

For better or for worse and *For richer, for poorer*. This portion of the vows reminds us of Paul's admonition to be content: "I have learned to be content whatever the circumstances. I know what it is to be in need, and I know what it is to have plenty. I have learned the secret of being content in any and every situation, whether well fed or hungry, whether living in plenty or in want. I can do all this through him who gives me strength" (Philippians 4:11-13). The status of your bank account should not be a reflection of your level of commitment.

In sickness and in health. We are back to Ephesians 5 again, this time with the emphasis on taking care of your mate with the same attention you give to yourself: "In this same way, husbands ought to love their wives as their own bodies. He who loves his wife loves himself. After all, no one ever hated their own body, but they feed and care for their body" (Ephesians 5:28-29). And for good measure, to understand this portion of the vow you could add on the golden rule! "Treat others the same way you want them to treat you" (Luke 6:31 NASB). How are you caring for the one you committed to? Is it with the same fervor and enthusiasm as you care for yourself and your own life?

Forsaking all others, I promise to keep only to you. In this passage from Malachi that deals with divorce, God repeats several times the admonition *do not be unfaithful.* "It is because the Lord is the witness between you and the wife of your youth. You have been unfaithful to her, though she is your partner, the wife of your marriage covenant. Has not the one God made you? You belong to him in body and spirit. And what does the one God seek? Godly offspring. So be on your guard, and do not be unfaithful to the wife of your youth" (Malachi 2:14-15). Faithfulness and exclusivity seem to be a "duh" that too many couples forget. Guard your marriage against infidelity.

From this day forward, until death do us part. When God made a covenant with Abram in Genesis 15, it was a blood covenant. The understanding was "If either of us break this vow, you can do to me what we have done to these animals we have just cut in two." There is no hiring a lawyer and looking for a loophole. Marriage was designed to last a lifetime, and if both of the partners are walking out their vows, death should be the one and only cause for separation.

Lord, help us remember and mean our wedding vows each and every day. Amen.

Poked with a Sword

The word of God is living and active and
sharper than any two-edged sword.
Hebrews 4:12 nasb

Ephesians 6:17 tells us that the Word of God is "the sword of the Spirit." This means that the Holy Spirit utilizes the words of the Bible to guide our steps. As you spend time reading and hearing the Bible, you will notice that some verses seem to jump off the page at you. Some of these verses help you feel better about yourself and about life. Others will disturb you and make you aware of some area of your life that God wants to change. As you pay attention to these verses, God interactively leads you toward His plan for you.

Here's an example of how this works. I (Bill) recently made a significant career transition in my life. For a man, this is often one of the hardest transitions in life. Men are highly motivated by success, after all! I was good at what I did and loved going to work. I also love what I am doing now, but it has required a high degree of learning and a whole new approach to career building. I was quite nervous about the process and was seeking confirmation from God. During this search, I read Psalm 32:8-9, which says, "I will instruct you and teach you in the way you should go; I will counsel you with my loving eye on you. Do not be like the horse or the mule, which have no understanding but must be controlled by bit and bridle or they will not come to you."

As soon as I read it, two thoughts flooded my mind. The first was, *Jesus has taken a personal interest in leading me through this transition in my life.* The second was, *I am stubborn and I need to give in to the change. I can either cooperate with this change and get through it relatively easily, or I can fight the change and experience a long and difficult year.*

I (Pam) was sitting in church one day during this transitional period in our life. Right in the middle of the sermon, the words, *This is the way; walk in it* (Isaiah 30:21) became vibrant in my mind. I cannot say that I heard them out loud but the words impacted me as if God had spoken them right into my ear. I had heard and read that passage many times, but it had never affected me like this before. I knew that God was using His Word to confirm Bill's call and give me confidence in the midst of this new transition in life.

You don't have to go looking for it. Simply stay consistent in exposing yourself to God's Word and God will poke you with the sword of the Spirit!

Lord, help me listen and respond to that light poke of truth that prods us closer to You and each other. Amen.

Why Are We Arguing?

Do everything without grumbling or arguing,
so that you may become blameless and pure,
"children of God without fault in a warped
and crooked generation."

PHILIPPIANS 2:14-15

In the small group Bible study for *Men Are Like Waffles—Women Are Like Spaghetti* we like to joke: "*Argument* (ar-gyou-ment). n. A discussion that occurs when you're right, but your mate just hasn't realized it yet."

We joke about arguments because it is so easy for everyone to find themselves in this rough place. We both grew up in homes that had a daily dose of disagreements. Once I (Pam) refereed an hour-long argument about whether the Chevy my dad was driving was a 1958 or a 1959! Couples can get into a cycle of disagreement in which everything becomes a point of contention. When we began our life together we could have repeated this unhealthy, destructive, time-wasting way of life but instead, we made a simple choice: Let God's Spirit select our words. We know this is a decision God applauds because He repeats the need over and again in the Bible:

- Psalm 141:3: "Set a guard over my mouth, LORD; keep watch over the door of my lips."

- Proverbs 13:3: "Those who guard their lips preserve their lives, but those who speak rashly will come to ruin."

- Proverbs 16:1: "To humans belong the plans of the heart, but from the LORD comes the proper answer of the tongue."

- Proverbs 21:23: "Those who guard their mouths and their tongues keep themselves from calamity."

- Proverbs 11:12: "Whoever derides their neighbor has no sense, but the one who has understanding holds their tongue."

- James 1:26: "Those who consider themselves religious and yet do not keep a tight rein on their tongues deceive themselves, and their religion is worthless."

- James 3:9-12: "With the tongue we praise our Lord and Father, and with it we curse human beings, who have been made in God's likeness. Out of the same mouth come praise and cursing. My brothers and sisters, this should not be. Can both fresh water and salt water flow from the same spring? My brothers and sisters, can a fig tree bear olives, or a grapevine bear figs? Neither can a salt spring produce fresh water."

Now that we have the principle in place to think and pray before we speak, let's look a little closer at the type of words to avoid and why:

- Proverbs 10:32: "The lips of the righteous know what finds favor, but the mouth of the wicked only what is perverse."

- Proverbs 4:24: "Keep your mouth free of perversity; keep corrupt talk far from your lips."

Perversity is words that are bent, crooked, or twisted, and "applied to persons involved in moral error."[19] You know exactly what you're doing when you twist words just to make your mate feel bad or look bad.

Corrupt talk is a pretty strong word meaning to debase, brutalize, demoralize, degrade, and ruin. This goes straight to the heart of your motive, the "why" of your word choice. What was in your heart when you said what you said? Try to keep Ephesians 5:4 in the front of your mind at all times, but *especially* when you're speaking to your spouse: "Nor should there be obscenity, foolish talk or coarse joking, which are out of place, but rather thanksgiving."

Obscenity means language that is filthy or shameful.

Foolish talk is silly or unnecessary.

Coarse joking is "humor" that is vulgar or nasty.

To sum this all up, ask yourself, "Would my mother, Nana, or pastor want to hear me say this?"

If not, it's a good bet that Jesus wouldn't want to hear it either. The couples that allow poor word choices to destroy their love (and ultimately their marriage) are tearing down their mates word by word, like a slow, steady drip.

One winter, a gentle rain started over our home. Its presence was welcome because we needed some moisture. When the rain hit at higher elevations it turned to snow, dusting the mountains that surround our home. It was a beautiful sight. But at the lower elevations where we live, on the side of a mountain, the gentle rain soon turned into a full-on storm. Soon it became a torrential downpour that pounded away at the mountainside. The puddles turned into streams and the streams became rushing rivers, creating a flash flood. And then, in a moment, the entire side of our yard slid down the hill. It was gone in what felt like a heartbeat, but in actuality, it eroded one tiny raindrop at a time. We just hadn't noticed the erosion until what was once ours was washed completely away. The devastation was immense.

In the same way, harsh words are like persistent raindrops. They might not feel like a big deal in the moment, but bit by bit they will wash away your love. Nitpicking, criticizing, critiquing, name-calling, fussing, and other cruel, unkind, inconsiderate, and mean words will ruin your marriage. The devastation will be immense. Remember: There is an art to the unsaid.

Lord, help each of us measure our words with love. If we err, let us apologize quickly and then encourage lavishly. Amen.

Choose the Opposite

*Walk by the Spirit, and you will not
gratify the desires of the flesh.*
GALATIANS 5:16

Inside every believer there is a war raging. It is the battle between the old self and the new self. The old self is empowered and directed by our natural human nature which is, by nature, selfish and deceptive. The new self is empowered and directed by the Holy Spirit and is, by nature, other-centered and relationally skillful. The apostle Paul lays out the contrast between the old self and the new self in his message to the Colossians:

But now you must also rid yourselves of all such things as these: anger, rage, malice, slander, and filthy language from your lips. Do not lie to each other, since you have taken off your old self with its practices and have put on the new self, which is being renewed in knowledge in the image of its Creator. Here there is no Gentile or Jew, circumcised or uncircumcised, barbarian, Scythian, slave or free, but Christ is all, and is in all. Therefore, as God's chosen people, holy and dearly loved, clothe yourselves with compassion, kindness, humility, gentleness and patience. Bear with each other and forgive one another if any of you has a grievance against someone. Forgive as the Lord forgave you. And over all these virtues put on love, which binds them all together in perfect unity. Let the peace of Christ rule in your hearts, since as members of one body you were called to peace. And be thankful (Colossians 3:8-15).

In your marriage, the Holy Spirit will use the contrast between these two natures to give you guidance. You will notice at times that your spouse is operating according to the old self. He or she may be angry or contentious or fearful, or any of a hundred other emotions in life. As this is happening, the Holy Spirit will prompt you to do the opposite. You will have a strange sense that you should respond to anger with gentleness, argument with peace, and hurtful words with compassion. It will go against your natural inclinations and you will probably resist it at first. It will feel abnormal. You're going to feel vulnerable when you "choose the opposite." Even if it feels strange, though, when you respond with gentleness you give the Holy Spirit the opportunity to change your spouse's heart and actions. You have probably noticed that it does not help to point out your spouse's bad behavior, even when you are right. It will create a fire in your relationship...but not the kind that leads to passion!

Try it and see what happens. Colossians 3 refers to this process as "putting off" the clothing of the old nature and "putting on" the clothing of the new. The point is that you have a choice, and the choice is usually irritatingly obvious. Your spouse's negative behavior is like a flashlight that points out the positive behavior the Holy Spirit wants to produce in you.

To function in the opposite spirit, ask yourself the question, "What is the opposite of this negative behavior?" Then scan through the fruit of the Spirit listed in Galatians 5:22-23 to clue you in to what Spirit-controlled choice you might need to make to rescue the relationship atmosphere: "The fruit of the Spirit is love, joy, peace, forbearance, kindness, goodness, faithfulness, gentleness and self-control."

So if you see out-of-control behavior, select self-control as your behavior. If you see harshness, choose gentleness. If you see flakiness, be faithful. If your mate is bad, be good; if rude, be kind; if impatient, choose patient longsuffering; if anxious, be the calming, peaceful voice in your household. If you spot anger, be positive, joyful, and pleasant. If your mate is acting cold and heartless, be loving, tender, and compassionate.

To accomplish this, you might need a little help. We suggest looking in two different places:

• *The thesaurus or another synonym finder.* If you feel the opposite trait needed is peace, go to the thesaurus and you will see words like *calm, quiet, still, silent, tranquil,* and *serene.*

Work your way through these behaviors and your mate should begin to calm down. At the very least, your choices will not be making the situation worse and your behavior will likely stop any escalation to the crisis.

• *Prayer.* Ask the Spirit of God to control your every word and every move. Let the whisper of the Spirit show you what to say and do (or not say or not do!).

When you choose the opposite of bad attitudes and bad behavior, it puts pressure on your mate to also give in to the Spirit's leading or influence.

There is no real downside to choosing the opposite. Even if it takes awhile to see change in your mate's poor choices, you will still be living and functioning with all those good traits of the Spirit, so you will be able to maintain love, joy, peace, patience, kindness, goodness, faithfulness, gentleness, and self-control in your home and marriage.

By making healthy choices, you won't be sucked into any toxic behaviors. If you are standing safely on the rock of the truth as your mate swims in the cesspool of toxic behavior, your choices will be the lifeline that will eventually rescue your mate. Today, ask for the Holy Spirit's power to help you choose the opposite!

Lord, help each of us make healthy choices even when our spouse elects the unhealthy. Let my choice to be controlled by Your Spirit be the lifesaver of love to my mate. Amen.

Day 55

Unusually Kind

The islanders showed us unusual kindness.
They built a fire and welcomed us all
because it was raining and cold.
ACTS 28:2

When Paul landed in Malta he said the islanders showed him "unusual kindness." Often Bill and I will look at each other after counseling an argumentative, hostile couple and say, "Why can't people just be kind?"

Colossians 3:12 tells us that as God's people we should be clothed with kindness. "Therefore, as God's chosen people, holy and dearly loved, clothe yourselves with compassion, kindness, humility, gentleness and patience." That means we can "put on" kindness. Just like we'd choose a shirt from the closet, pull it out, and put it on, we can choose to be kind. That's all romance really is—a lifetime and life-*style* of thoughtful kindness. Today, your job is to say or do something that is encouraging. Be *unusually* kind.

Love is a verb. It causes you to say and do things that are unusually kind. One of the epic stories from our own love life happened on our honeymoon when Bill showed unusual kindness. I (Pam) had just stepped from the shower and was looking into the mirror. I began to criticize my body. Bill was sitting on the bed, admiring his new wife. As I would comment on an area I thought needed improving, Bill began to panic. He was afraid I would continue to point out my shortcomings and then get depressed, and sex would be out of the question! I went on for a few minutes until he could stand it no longer. He was angry that I would put down his choice of a wife. I was not only tearing myself down but undermining Bill's taste. But instead of saying something in anger, he prayed, "God, I could do a better job than that mirror!"

He stood up, wrapped his arms around me, and told me to look straight into his eyes. He very seriously and very lovingly said, "I will be your mirror. My eyes will reflect your beauty. You are beautiful, Pamela. You are perfect, and if you ever doubt it, come stand before me. The mirror of my eyes will tell you the true story. You are perfect for me. If I have to throw away every mirror in the house to get you to believe me, I will! From now on, let me be your mirror!"[20]

Every time we tell this story in a conference, one of two things happens. Either the audience breaks out in spontaneous applause or we hear an "Ooooh!" in unison from the listeners. I think the reason why this happens it that this story captures what it means to be unusually kind. That story went on to be the inspiration for a song called "I Will Be Your Mirror" by Boomer and Lisa Reiff. That song then turned into a music video for our *Men Are Like Waffles— Women Are Like Spaghetti* small group curriculum. Today that song is sung at many weddings, and the story moves others to become unusually kind as well.

But more important than this epic story is the powerful healing that happened in my heart that day. My heart had been shattered by the harsh words and actions of my father, who was too broken to love in a way that reflected God's unusually kind character. That day, at the very beginning of our married life, God gave Bill unusually kind words that helped heal my wounded spirit.

There is a line in the song "I Will Be Your Mirror" that captures what happened in me when I heard those unusually kind words:

And now she looks back on her life
at all the years that have come and gone,
and she knows the gift he gave that day
became the ground she's walked upon.

Those unusually kind words laid the foundation for an usually strong love and an unusually powerful ministry to others who are looking for this same kind of epic love. But it isn't just words that show unusual kindness. Actions often speak even louder than words. Bill also loved me with unusual kindness when he:

- worked two jobs for many years so I could be a stay-at-home mother when our children were small.

- got up with the babies in the middle of the night so I could sleep.

- stopped what he was doing to fix my computer—or my feelings (more times than I can count!).

- hammered a home together while he was working full-time.

- was a fully engaged parent who often thanked me for being a mom who cared.

And our marriage worked because I wanted to boomerang the same unusual kindness right back to him. Your marriage can show the same kind of superhuman kindness when you let the Holy Spirit work in and through you. So don't just do the expected. This week, go for the unexpected—be unusually kind!

Lord, help me seek to be unusually kind. Help me go above and beyond for my mate. Amen.

Willing Partner

I always pray with joy because of your partnership in the gospel from the first day until now, being confident of this, that he who began a good work in you will carry it on to completion until the day of Christ Jesus.

Philippians 1:4-6

We get caught up on a regular basis thinking we have to be spectacular. We watch an athletic contest on TV and we think we need to be like one of the superstars on the field. We flip through magazines and think we should look like the models. We watch the news and think we should be on top of every story and situation. We watch our grandkids play and think that we need to be an awesome "Nana" and "Poppa" if we want them to reach their potential. We find it easy to put expectations on ourselves and conclude it is all up to us as a couple.

Then we read passages such as Philippians 1:5 and Isaiah 6 and are reminded that life is a partnership. We are full partners in our marriage, so we need to do our best every day with full focus and energy. We also need to do our best to learn new skills so we can maximize our effectiveness as a couple. But we have a partner who makes a much bigger contribution than we could ever imagine:

I saw the Lord, high and exalted, seated on a throne; and the train of his robe filled the temple. Above him were seraphim…And they were calling to one another: "Holy, holy, holy is the LORD Almighty; the whole earth is full of his glory." At the sound of their voices the doorposts and thresholds shook and the temple was filled with smoke (Isaiah 6:1-4).

What a great reminder that we serve an awesome

God. He is more powerful, authoritative, compassionate, and capable than anyone else we know. When He shows up, mountains tremble. Our first reaction when we read this today was to say, "We are with Him!"

Our second reaction was to realize that He doesn't really need our help. Our abilities look simple and childlike compared to His. Our words sound immature, our thoughts appear undeveloped, and our strength looks puny. But still, He has called us to be partners: "Then I heard the voice of the Lord saying, 'Whom shall I send? And who will go for us?'" (Isaiah 6:8). God is looking for people who are willing to be His representatives.

This is why your example as a couple impacts others simply because you are in love. For example, Tom and Barbara seem to be an ordinary couple but their love gave us confidence. We both grew up in homes with significantly unhealthy patterns and were concerned about whether we could avoid those same patterns in our relationship. Watching Tom and Barbara in action convinced us that a better way was possible.

Or take Mark and Sheri. They are another couple who would likely describe themselves as commonplace, but their love toward us felt spectacular. They asked us to house-sit when we were newlyweds, pregnant with our first child and basically homeless for a summer while we were interning for six weeks in youth work. The genuine love and laughter they shared with each other and generosity toward us changed the way we think about influencing others. We know that humor and generously giving to others helps people grow because we saw it in them.

In the same way, others are watching you and getting stronger because of your example. It isn't because you are so talented. It is because you are in partnership with a miracle-working God. He doesn't need help but He wants our involvement. All we have to be is willing. He will provide the message, the strength, and the wisdom. He is simply looking for people who want to be involved in His plan to show the world His love, grace, purpose, and compassion. Isaiah got it right when he merely said, "Here am I. Send me!" (verse 8).

Day 57

What Love!

Love never fails.
1 CORINTHIANS 13:8

It is not in our power that we can succeed at love. Rather, it is depending on God's perfect love that will make your love victorious.

Romans 8:37-39 explains it this way:

We are more than conquerors through him who loved us. For I am convinced that neither death nor life, neither angels nor demons, neither the present nor the future, nor any powers, neither height nor depth, nor anything else in all creation, will be able to separate us from the love of God that is in Christ Jesus our Lord.

God needed us to know that nothing, absolutely positively *nothing*, could separate us from the source of love—God Himself. Because He promised this, we can stand confident in our frail, fallible human relationships. As mere mortals, we are imperfect, but when fused with God's perfect love, we can be empowered to love in His same manner. The impossible becomes possible because of this ever-powerful spring of eternally secure love.

We wrote a book called *Love, Honor, and Forgive*, and in it we shared numerous stories of couples in rough water, separated or even divorced, who beat all the odds and came back together to be victorious in love. One critic of the book said we'd made up all these stories. It just wasn't possible that there were real couples like this! She dismissed them as fable or fiction. However, we interviewed each and every one of those couples. They are very real, and their love is a miracle.

Each of us feels the need of a miracle of love at some point in time. It is then God can step in and free us, release us, and unchain us, and then rework, rebuild, and renew love with His power!

When we are at an impasse in our love life, we go back to God's definition of love in 1 Corinthians 13. We read it and ask, "Where am I lacking in love?" Notice that we said, "Where am *I* lacking." If love is to be rekindled the fuel must be added from our own hand. We cannot demand change from our mate because we do not control our mate; we only control ourselves. We must be willing to be empowered by God's Holy Spirit and His power to love through us!

Let's look at God's definition of love from 1 Corinthians 13:4-8:

Love is patient, love is kind. It does not envy, it does not boast, it is not proud. It does not dishonor others, it is not self-seeking, it is not easily angered, it keeps no record of wrongs. Love does not delight in evil but rejoices with the truth. It always protects, always trusts, always hopes, always perseveres. Love never fails.

The way to have a more loving relationship is to be more loving yourself! When love is not working, ask yourself which part of love you are lacking. Then

ask God to send His ability to love to work through
you. Which of these parts of love might you need
right now?

- Patience: Does your marriage need you to have
  an enduring passion or a willingness to wait?

- Kindness: Are you seeking to be gentle in your
  behavior?

- Does not envy: Are you exhibiting a love that
  does not boil over with jealousy?

- Does not boast: Are you refusing to brag about
  yourself and your own accomplishments?

- Not proud: Are you puffing yourself up or are
  you electing to be humble?

- Does not dishonor others: Is your love rude,
  indecent, impolite, uncouth, or offensive? Can
  you instead seek to be well-mannered and
  gracious?

- Not self-seeking: Are you looking only after
  your own interests, or can you keep the best
  interests of your mate in mind?

- Not easily angered: Are you easily irritated or
  are you willing to expunge sharpness from
  your spirit?

- Keeps no records of wrongs: Are you recording your mate's faults and mistakes in a ledger book? Or will you choose to throw that ledger on the trash heap?

- Does not rejoice in evil: Are you rejoicing when evil triumphs, or are you seeking to be honest, forthcoming, and straightforward with kindness and tact?

- Rejoices in the truth: Can you find joy in everything that is true, even when the truth might shine a light into areas that need growth in your own life?

- Protects: Do you cover your mate like a roof, protecting him or her against the storms of life?

- Trusts: Do you have faith in your spouse without being gullible?

- Hopes: Are you looking on the bright side of every situation? Finding the silver lining in every stormy day? Can you choose to be positive when you feel like despairing?

- Perseveres: Are you able to carry on like a stouthearted soldier aiming for a higher call?

- Never fails: Are you seeking to have a love that can survive any and every attack upon it?

Lord, help us understand what love is. Show us the source and power of love that is found only in You. Help us tap into who You are when we lack an element of love. Amen.

The Game

*And let us run with perseverance the race
marked out for us, fixing our eyes on Jesus,
the pioneer and perfecter of faith. For the joy
set before him he endured the cross, scorning
its shame, and sat down at the right hand of
the throne of God. Consider him who endured
such opposition from sinners, so that you will
not grow weary and lose heart. In your struggle
against sin, you have not yet resisted to the
point of shedding your blood.*
HEBREWS 12:1-4

My all-time favorite message from my husband's 15-plus years as a senior pastor is on James
1:2-8, when he talks about *the struggle of being in the*

game. It dovetails with the encouragement to keep running the race, even—especially—when it's a struggle, that we see in today's passage from the book of Hebrews.

Picture the field of athletic competition or the Olympic games. As James describes it in verses 2-4, we believers experience the same types of struggles as athletes: "Consider it pure joy, my brothers and sisters, whenever you face trials of many kinds, because you know that the testing of your faith produces perseverance. Let perseverance finish its work so that you may be mature and complete, not lacking anything."

In verse 3, *testing* means to be tested and then approved. Picture yourself being drafted for a football team. The coaches know your record, are familiar with your bio and stats, and have watched films of your games—and then they select you! You have been tested and approved. So the struggles mentioned here are not just the general struggles of life. They are the specific struggles that go along with being willing to be "on the field." These are the challenges that make you bigger, faster, and stronger spiritually so you will be prepared to face even greater challenges ahead. These struggles come to couples who have prayed, "Yes, Lord, use our love as a light to show the world what Your love really looks like."

Every key word in this section is about athletics:

In verse 4, *mature and complete* carries the sense of being in sync with God. It has the force of being in line with the plan and instructions of the coach. Then *complete* is the term for "complete in all its parts," or "entirely complete." This means that every part of your body must be ready for competition. Finally, the term *lacking* means "to be left behind." This word means that any weak areas that would otherwise hold you back have been treated and trained.

Athletes understand the need for endurance and are not surprised by the struggle of competition. They willingly go through rigorous workouts to develop endurance because they recognize that games are always won in the fourth quarter, and every winner is determined at the finish line! They therefore welcome the struggle that gives them the ability to compete. In the same way, any believer, any couple, who want to make a difference in the world for Christ will experience trying circumstances that will pave the way for further influence.

In our life, the struggle of being in the game comes from being on the treadmill of constant travel, merciless deadlines, and handling the ever-pressing needs of people. We often sacrifice time with each other to help rescue others experiencing crisis in their relationships. But we never forget that it's worth it!

Here's a good way of looking at it. All three of our sons played football, and two received college scholarships to play. What they always wanted was game time—not bench-warming time! In high school, they would often play both offense and defense. This meant that by the end of the game they were exhausted, but thrilled. Physically they were spent, but emotionally they were jazzed from all the wonderful opportunities to perform in the game.

We're the same way—we want game time! And that is why our marriage has lasted for over 32 years. Are we tired? Physically, yes, most of the time.

Tired of the opportunity or tired of the game? Not a chance!

Join us in our cause to get off the bench and get in the game! Ask God to make your marriage a reflection of His love and grace. Look for ways to serve God together as a couple. If you do, at the end of the game, when the final whistle blows, you will hear, "Well done, good and faithful servant!" Scoreboard, baby!

Lord, help us be willing to serve You as a couple all the way until the final whistle blows. Amen.

Endnotes

1 Amber Madison, "Sex and Exercise: Sexercise?" *CollegeSexperts* (blog), August 22, 2003, http://collegesexperts.blogspot.com/.

2 Also cited in: Bill and Pam Farrel, *Red-Hot Monogamy* (Eugene, OR: Harvest House Publishers, 2006), 21-22.

3 Janet Lee, "Lifestyle Q&A," *GymAmerica,* http://wwwgymamerica .com/www/misc/MagazineQA.aspx?cid=729.

4 Adapted from: Pam Farrel, *52 Ways to Wow Your Husband* (Eugene, OR: Harvest House Publishers, 2011), 22-23.

5 Richard Glotzer and Anne Cairns Federlein. "Miles That Bind: Commuter Marriage and Family Strengths." *Michigan Family Review* 12, no. 1 (2007), under "Two Case Studies in Commuter Marriage: Anne's Story."

6 James A. Swanson, *Dictionary of Biblical Languages with Semantic Domains: Greek (New Testament)* (Bellingham, WA: Logos Research Systems, Inc., 1997), electronic edition.

7 "Redbook Magazine's 'America's Hottest Husband,'" *The Talk,* CBS, January 20, 2012, http://www.cbs.com/show/the_talk/ video/2188846560/the-talk-redbook-magazine-s-america-s- hottest-husband-.

8 *Strong's Greek and Hebrew Dictionary,* s.v. "5011, *tapeinos*."

9 "How Does a Pressure Cooker Work?" *Miss Vickie's Pressure Cooker Recipes,* accessed March 8, 2012, http://missvickie.com/ workshop/howdoesit.html.

10 John Walvoord and Roy Zuck, eds., *The Bible Knowledge Commentary: An Exposition of the Scriptures* (Colorado Springs: David C. Cook, 1983), s.v. "Philippians 1:7."

11 Laurie Puhn, "Love and Sex: The Secrets of Close Couples," *Women's Health Magazine,* January/February 2011, 106.

12 Nathan Stone, *Names of God* (Chicago: Moody Press, 1944), 60.

13 A.W. Tozer, *The Knowledge of the Holy* (New York: Harper Collins, 1961), 1.

14 Henry Blackaby and Claude King, *Experiencing God* (Nashville: B&H Publishing Group, 2009), 209.

15 Pam Farrel, *Becoming a Brave New Woman* (Eugene, OR: Harvest House Publishers, 2012), 15.

16 I. Howard Marshall et al., eds., *New Bible Dictionary*, 3rd ed. (Downers Grove, IL: InterVarsity Press, 1996), 217.

17 Vicki Heath, *Don't Quit Get Fit: Overcoming the 4 Fitness Killers* (Delight, AR: Gospel Light, 2011), 81.

18 This story is also related in: Bill and Pam Farrel, *The Marriage Code* (Eugene, OR: Harvest House Publishers, 2010), 242-43.

19 Charles W. Draper et al., eds., *Holman Illustrated Bible Dictionary* (Nashville, TN: Holman Bible Publishers, 2003), 1280.

20 This story is also related in: Bill and Pam Farrel, *Men are Like Waffles—Women are Like Spaghetti* (Eugene, OR: Harvest House Publishers, 2000), 21.